# *Horse Farms and Horse Tales*
## *of the Bluegrass*

**Wilma Clapp**

# Acknowledgements

Without the assistance, knowledge, expertise, and time that was so freely given by so many people, this book could not have been written. At each farm and business I visited, everyone graciously shared their knowledge of and love for what they do. Thanks for reading and rereading and providing guidance where needed. Your help was invaluable.

During the course of researching this book, I had the pleasure of meeting Elizabeth Lampton, owner, with her husband, Dinwiddie, of Elmendorf Farm. She was gracious, welcoming, and charming, providing information and encouragement. I came away from our meetings convinced that she truly loved three things – her husband, her horses, and Elmendorf. Tragically, on March 22, 2008, Mrs. Lampton died as a result of a carriage accident on her beloved Elmendorf. This book is dedicated to her.

# Table of Contents

# Introduction

Almost everyone agrees that the Bluegrass region of Kentucky is the horse industry's capital. It is also a unique and beautiful area that welcomes thousands of visitors each year. Although how this particular region arrived at such a position of prominence is disputed, most authorities agree that it was not just one incident, but a series of natural and historic events that led to this region becoming the headquarters of the racing world.

In many ways, fate played as big a role as any in determining the horse industry's position in Kentucky. Before the American colonies declared their political independence, blooded horses were routinely imported from England into Virginia, the first of the colonies to bring Thoroughbreds to the area. When early Virginians and other colonists began to migrate westward, Kentucky offered miles of navigable waters and a pass through the mountains that allowed an influx of pioneers and their stock into the area. The horses brought into Kentucky were extraordinarily hardy, survivors of both the journey from England into the colonies and the trip from the colonies into Kentucky.

Once in Kentucky, immigrants found limestone-based soil, lush grasses, and an abundance of mineral-laden water—all of which contribute to the development of strong, healthy horses. These early horsemen decided to stay in the area to take advantage of the state's natural bounties. By the late 1700's, horses were being raced in the streets, and in 1797 Kentucky's first Jockey Club was founded in Lexington.

Until the Civil War, Kentucky had developed only a moderately-successful equine industry. However, as Kentucky remained neutral during the war, it suffered less physical damage than did other Southern states and land values remained attractive. As a result, many great horses were brought into the region by wealthy men seeking a more favorable location for their breeding stock. Once settled, they established some of the world's premier horse farms. Today, almost 200 of these farms are located in Fayette County. This book tells the story of a few of these great farms and some of the horses that live on them.

Section one provides in-depth information on several area farms considered to be representative of the different types of horse farm found in the Bluegrass region. Farm history, current plans, and tales of some of the farm's most famous and infamous inhabitants are included.

Section two contains stories about horses that were bred or foaled in the region. Although many of these horses have long since passed on, they remain legend to their many admirers. These horses were some of the best of the very best and have records to prove it

Section three provides information on area attractions such as Keeneland and The Red Mile racetracks, and other peripheral equine-related businesses such as the North American Racing Academy. A map of these places is included in the last section, along with a glossary of equine terms.

This book is an attempt to record a bit of the history and the stories surrounding the Bluegrass region's horse world. It can be used as part of a self-guided tour or in conjunction with an organized tour provided by local touring agencies. Some of the farms featured in the book have histories dating back to Kentucky's early statehood; some are fairly recent additions to the racing scene. A few have absentee owners; others are family-owned and operated. All of them, however, have one thing in common: they have consistently produced outstanding horses.

*Lane's End stallion barn*

# Horse Farms of Note

# Calumet Farm

On March 26, 1992, Lexingtonians and racehorse fans across the country breathed a collective sigh of relief when it was announced that horseman Henryk deKwiatkowski had purchased bankrupt Calumet Farm at public auction. He received a standing ovation after the auction when he pledged that he would change "not a whisker[1]" of the historic showplace. Obviously, Calumet's white plank fences and bright red and white barns mean a lot to many different people.

For local residents, Calumet is the epitome of Bluegrass culture, a landmark that symbolizes the best of the Bluegrass. For racehorse fans, the name Calumet is synonymous with great Thoroughbred horses: the farm has produced two Triple Crown winners and an unprecedented eight Kentucky Derby winners. For visitors flying into Lexington's Bluegrass Airport, Calumet is the "Welcome to Kentucky" sign, a visible promise of an enjoyable and hospitable visit. Although the farm has been a part of Fayette County since 1924, the wealth which built this dynasty was made not with Thoroughbred horses, but with profits from a baking powder invented in Chicago.

In the early 1900's when biscuits were still made from "scratch," William Wright invented a better baking powder. He named the baking powder Calumet, designed a red and white can, and founded the Calumet Baking Powder company. Later, Wright's son, Warren, joined the company and sales and profits soared.

The elder Wright was a Standardbred enthusiast and as profits from the company rose, he was able indulge his passion. In 1924 he bought the Fairland Farm in Lexington, Kentucky, renamed it Calumet, and moved his family and Standardbreds to Kentucky. Shortly before the Depression, the Wrights sold their interest in the baking powder company, and Wright was able to devote his full attention to his hobby-turned-business Standardbred operation.

William Wright died in 1931. Although Warren inherited the 900-acre family farm, he did not inherit his father's love of Standardbreds, preferring Thoroughbred horses instead, and he rapidly converted the Kentucky farm to a Thoroughbred operation. He was either a very clever horse trader, incredibly lucky, or both.

Wright's first broodmare, Nellie Morse, was one of the few fillies to win the Preakness Stakes. Nellie Morse produced Nellie Flag, who became a champion two-year-old in 1934, and upon retirement, she produced a champion mare and several outstanding runners. When Wright purchased his first stallion, he bought a $14,000 yearling, Bull Lea, who became an outstanding sire and the foundation for Calumet's success. (Before his death in 1964 at the age of 29, Bull Lea sired,

*Architectural Detail on Main Residence*

among others, Twilight Tear, Coaltown, and Citation.) In 1939 when a trainer was needed, Wright hired Ben A. Jones, who became the trainer of such greats as Whirlaway and Citation, both Triple Crown winners and the first horses to earn a half million and a million dollars, respectively.

Warren Wright, Sr., died in 1950, and the bulk of his estate went into trusts for his widow, Lucille, and their son, Warren, Jr. Under the terms of the will, Lucille was to control Calumet during her life and at her death, the farm was to pass to Warren, Jr. Two years later Lucille married Rear Admiral Gene Markey, Hollywood writer and film producer, and they successfully continued the management of the farm. During this period, 77 stakes winners were bred, and racehorse greats such as Forward Pass, Tim Tam, Iron Liege, and Alydar became part of Calumet's racing string.

In 1978, the Markeys had almost reached the age when it would become physically impossible to go to the track, and decided to attend what was to be their last race during Keeneland's spring meet, which coincided with Alydar's final pre-Derby race. When jockey Jorge Velasquez rode Alydar over to present him to his elderly owners, the horse spontaneously bowed to his mistress and, as a bonus, won the

*Calumet Farm*

3301 Versailles Road
Lexington, KY 40510
(859) 231-8272
www.calumetfarm.com

race by an overwhelming 13-1/4 length margin.

Gene Markey died in 1980 and Mrs. Markey followed two years later. Control of the farm fell to the heirs of Warren Wright, Jr., who had died in 1978 at the age of 58. Although Warren, Jr., was survived by his widow, Bertha, and four children, none of his heirs played an active role in Calumet's management. Instead J. T. Lundy, Warren's son-in-law, became president of Calumet, even though his previous experience was at best minimal.

With Lundy in control, changes in key personnel were made and large sums of money spent. The office and house were extensively renovated, a jet was leased at a cost of $500,000 a year, entertainment and travel expenditures soared, and millions were spent on horses. The farm might have been able to withstand this monetary drain, except that tax laws, once favorable to the horse industry, underwent a drastic change in the mid-'80s. These new tax laws, coupled with an economic recession, drove horse farms across the country into financial chaos, and Calumet was no exception.

The biggest disaster to hit Calumet, however, happened in November 1990, when Alydar kicked the wall of his stable, broke his leg, and had to be destroyed. This blow was the straw that broke Calumet's economic back.

At the time of Mrs. Markey s death in 1982, Calumet was debt-free, the farm was in good repair, and Alydar, retired to stud, had become the world's leading sire. In 1991, less than nine years later, Alydar was dead, there were no horses on the farm, and Calumet owed its creditors more than $127 million.

In early 1991 Lundy was replaced as president, but his successor found Calumet to be in total financial ruin. By July the farm was in bankruptcy and in March 1992 sold at public auction.

The farm's new owner, Henryk deKwiatkowski, paid $17,000,000 for the nucleus of the farm—763 acres—on which the main house is located. Built in 1930 and renovated in 1983, the house contains 14 rooms, 6 full- and two half-baths. Adjacent to the house is a tennis court and a swimming pool. There are eight other houses on the farm, 15 barns, a veterinary clinic, and a three-quarter mile training track.

Mr. deKwiatkowski died in March 2003. His children are the beneficiaries of a trust, based in the Bahamas that now owns and manages Calumet.

# Castleton Lyons

## Castleton Lyons

2469 Ironworks Pike
Lexington, KY
(859) 455-9222
www.castletonlyons.com

Ironworks Pike, one of the most picturesque roads in Fayette County, owes much of its appeal to the beauty of historic Castleton Lyons Farm. Surrounded by well-maintained stone fences, this 2,000-acre farm has an outstanding record in almost all facets of the horse industry, from the Thoroughbreds of the Breckinridges to the Standardbreds of the Van Lenneps. Not only is it rich in equine history, but its origins can be traced to 1790, two years before Kentucky was granted statehood.  It was then that John Breckinridge, United States Senator and Attorney General under Thomas Jefferson, began the development of what was to become Castleton Lyons.

A Virginia native, John Breckinridge was attracted to the rich lands of Kentucky and ultimately acquired more than 2,000 acres of prime Bluegrass farmland, which he named Cabell's Dale for his

*Castleton Lyons Entrance*

wife, Mary Cabell Breckinridge. Although he raised hemp, corn, and other livestock on the farm, he loved horses, and at his death in 1806, he owned 128 Thoroughbreds. (His devoted wife was alleged to be so distraught at his death that she not only went bald, but went blind as well, having literally "cried her eyes out.")

In 1812 when she was 16 years old, Breckinridge's daughter, Mary Ann, married David Castleman. She died four years later during the birth of their first child. As the child also died within a few years, Castleman became the sole beneficiary of Mary Ann's estate.

In 1825 Castleman married his deceased wife's cousin, who bore him 11 children. Castleton at the time consisted of horse barns and paddocks for Castleman's saddlers, a deer park, orchards, a greenhouse, a 10-acre lawn and nine slaves to care for the household. Two houses in which slaves

were quartered are still maintained by the farm, and an antebellum brick hemp house can be seen at the intersection of Newtown and Ironworks Pikes. Located just down the road on Ironworks Pike is the Mt. Horeb Presbyterian Church: Castleman served as an elder in the church and donated the land on which the church now stands.

Castleman designed and constructed the farm's elegant Greek Revival style mansion in 1840. The entrance hall is 14 feet wide and 42 feet long, and at the end of the hall is a beautiful spiral stairway. Four massive doors open into the drawing room, which has large gilt mirrors over the mantels. There is a reception room, library, and a lavish dining room with polished hardwood floors covered with oriental rugs.

After Castleman's death in 1852, ownership of the farm changed many times. (The farm once sold for $111 per acre.) Generally, when the owners changed, the breed of horses changed as well—from saddlers to trotters to Thoroughbreds to Saddlebreds to Standardbreds and back to Thoroughbreds. The number of champions and leading sires of all breeds that Castleton has produced is remarkable. During James Keene's ownership (1893 to 1911), the farm became one of the most celebrated Thoroughbred farms in the United States, with 113 stakes winners in 15 years, including the magnificent Domino.

In 1911 David Look, who raised trotters, bought Castleton, and he produced the top broodmare of the day, Emily Ellen. Following Look's death, the farm was purchased by Mrs. Frances Dodge Johnson, whose Dodge Stables in Michigan were known as one of the nation's principal show rings. She established the Dodge Stable Division of Castleton Farm, where noted trainer Earl Teater produced exceptional show horses. At the corner of Iron Works and Mt. Horeb Roads there is a state historical marker honoring one of her horses, Wing Commander, possibly the world's most famous five-gaited saddle horse.

In 1949 Frances Johnson married Frederick Van Lennep, initiator of the Breeder's Crown of Racing and the American Horse Council. Together the Van Lenneps developed and improved the farm. Six tenant houses were added, as well as a large, horseshoe-shaped swimming pool. Many fine show horses contributed to Castleton's large trophy and blue ribbon collection during this period. Although Mrs. Van Lennep died in 1971, the show horse division was operated until 1975 when Castleton returned to the exclusive business of raising Standardbred horses. Under Mr.

*Bret Hanover Statue*

*Restored Slave Quarters*

Van Lennep's guidance, Castleton continued its tradition of excellence and innovation. His death in 1987 was a great loss not only to Castleton, but to the horse industry, as well.

In 2001, Dr. Tony Ryan purchased the farm and under his direction, major renovations were made, including returning the farm to its Thoroughbred roots and changing the name to Castleton Lyons. A long-time supporter of the arts, in 2006 Dr. Ryan was part of the inauguration of the Castleton Lyons-Thoroughbred Times Book Award, which recognizes outstanding literary works relating to the Thoroughbred industry.

Dr. Ryan died in October 2007, but his sons, who have been involved with the farm since its purchase, will continue the operation. The farm stands many well-known stallions, and is also a first-class boarding operation.

*For a horse to be considered truly white, he must have blue eyes, pink skin, and a white coat with no dark hairs. There was such a horse in Germany in 1925, but statisticians had calculated that the odds of another white horse being born were two to three million to one, and that the odds of two white horses being born on the same farm were four trillion to one. However, in 1963, a white horse was born in France. Even more improbable, however, was that also in 1963 both a white colt and a white filly, each sired by a chestnut, were born on the Patchen Wilkes Farm in Lexington, Kentucky. As the colt later displayed reddish freckles on his chest, he was registered by the Jockey Club as a roan. The filly, however, appropriately named* White Beauty, *was registered by the Jockey Club as a white horse, and is the only one to date to be classified as white.*

# Clovelly Farm

## Clovelly Farm

820 Hughes Lane
Lexington, KY 40511
(859) 299-5131

Clovelly Farm, one of the oldest farms in the Bluegrass region, was once a part of James Haggin's sprawling Elmendorf Farm. By 1959, however, only 1,287 of the original Elmendorf acreage remained. These were divided into three separate tracts: one tract kept the Elmendorf name, one became Normandy Farm, and the other became Clovelly. Although Clovelly shares the history of the Elmendorf/Haggin era, it is still unique in many respects.

Clovelly is more informal than its illustrious ancestor. Although gracious and traditional in design, most of the buildings appear more utilitarian and are constructed of clapboard rather than stone. There is no formal "main house;" owner Robin Scully is a British citizen who spends the majority of his time in the United Kingdom. There is

a charming guest house overlooking a large lake; a smaller house, built in the 1800's, which once housed the resident trainer; and eight other houses which house the farm's employees, including retired farm manager Lars LaCour. In 1928 a dormitory, since divided into two apartments, was built for jockeys and exercise boys. Located just below the stable area is a small log cabin which once housed two slave families.

All of the barns on the farm are white clapboard with dark green trim, including the famous circular barn built in the late 1920's by Joseph Widener. This 38-stall barn is dotted with European-style, porcelain good-luck charms, later added by Mr. Scully. A winged Pegasus,

*Winged Horse on Barn*

doves, and peacocks are stationed at various points across the roof.

Clovelly is unique in its landscaping as well. Although many horse farm owners in the Bluegrass area have spent thousands of dollars planting hundreds of trees, the trees at Clovelly are incomparable. Beginning at the farm's main entrance, hundreds of giant sycamore trees form a canopy that provides shade across the farm. And instead of following a straight line, as is traditional on most farms, the road through Clovelly winds around the trees.

When Clovelly was separated from Elmendorf, it was first purchased by Thomas Bennett, who later sold the property to John Gaines. Gaines then sold it to Thomas Eaton who kept it for a couple of years, before selling it in 1965 to its present owner. Scully already owned 75 acres on Paris Pike, and in 1967 purchased an additional 167 acres from Normandy Farm. In 1989 he added 200 acres from Spendthrift Farm, which raised Clovelly's total acreage to the approximately 700 acres that it is today.

Outstanding stakes winners that have been bred at Clovelly include Silver Hawk, Cricket Ball, Alkaased, record-setting winner of the 2005 Japan Cup, and 2003 Breeders' Cup Classic winner Pleasantly Perfect, who went on the next year to win the Dubai World Cup. Before his retirement to Lanes End farm in 2004, his winnings topped over $7.5 million dollars.

Many fine mares have also been raised at Clovelly, and upon their death they are returned to the farm for burial. The farm's first mare, Lady Lufton, stakes winner Rajput Princess, Caterina, and champions Yahabeebe and Ancient Regime are all buried on the farm. The farm, now managed by Jeff Ownby, is currently home to about 34 mares, 18 of which are owned by Clovelly.

*According to Kentucky's rules of racing, there are two—and only two—drugs that can be administered to a horse before a race: Butazolidin (also known as bute) and Lasix. Bute is a non-steroidal anti-inflammatory drug given to horses with sore or injured joints (somewhat similar to an athlete taking ibuprofen prior to a race). Lasix is a diuretic given to prevent nose bleeds in "bleeders" (horses whose noses tend to bleed when under physical stress).*

*Restored 2-Family Slave Quarters*

# Darby Dan Farm

With gently rolling fields, white plank fence, quietly grazing Thoroughbreds, and a beautiful antebellum mansion, Darby Dan Farm is the quintessential Bluegrass horse farm. Although it can trace its roots back to 1788, the land which made up Darby Dan, King Ranch, and Mare Haven farms was not converted to a Thoroughbred operation until 1905, when Colonel Edward R. Bradley leased Ash Grove Farm and developed one of the most influential Thoroughbred breeding farms in the history of the industry.

Col. Bradley was born in Johnstown, Pennsylvania, the son of Irish immigrant parents. He began his career in the steel mills of Pittsburgh, but at the age of 14 migrated to the west where he found his fortune. Bradley

*Darby Dan Entrance*

*Statue of Black Toney*

worked many jobs while drifting across the west, including gold prospector, cowboy, and dishwasher. In the 1880's, however, he took up professional gambling, and became a Memphis, Tennessee, bookmaker. He and his brother, John, soon acquired interests in gambling casinos in both New Jersey and Long Island. By 1898 they had acquired and were operating the opulent, and illegal, Beach Club gambling establishment in Palm Beach, Florida. Known as "the Monte Carlo of America," the club became the spot for high rollers to meet and play for large stakes. It was said that Bradley would bet on anything, including the weather, and that he proudly listed his profession on tax returns as "Gambler."

In 1905, Bradley became an avid horse owner, breeder, and racer. The pursuit of

13

breeding a Kentucky Derby winner was the third great passion of his life (the first being his wife, Agnes, and the second, gambling). He leased, and then bought, Ash Grove Farm, renaming it Idle Hour Stock Farm. He continued to add acreage until the farm had grown to almost 1,700 acres. He also began breeding some of the greatest horses the racetrack has ever seen. His horses won four Kentucky Derbys, a record for the day, and twice his entries ran both first and second in this prestigious race. He bred 127 stakes winners, 14 champions, and one Horse of the Year, Busher, in 1945. His first great stallion, Black Toney, (for which he paid $1,600 in 1912) produced several winners, including Bimelech, sired by Black Toney when he was 25. In 1940 Bimelech ran second in the Kentucky Derby, but won both the Preakness and Belmont Stakes. (A statue of Black Toney is the centerpiece of Darby Dan's horse cemetery.)

Bradley spared no expense for his horses. He believed in the recuperative powers of sunshine and built a "sun barn" with a roof that could be opened for horses recovering from the stresses of the track. He constructed a tunnel under Old Frankfort Pike so that his horses could cross safely. When several of his horses were diagnosed as having severe astigmatism, Bradley bought them outrageously-priced eyeglasses. (Unfortunately, the first horse to try the glasses became so frightened at his new view of the world that he bolted and ran, hospitalizing his jockey for more than a month. The experiment was not repeated.)

The main house at Darby Dan, built in 1828, was remodeled to suit the Colonel and was specifically designed so that he could watch his horses from either the glass-enclosed front porch or from his office. The lower level of the house contains the trophy room, where the farm's green and white racing silks are showcased, and the dining and living areas, where pictures of the farm's champion horses are displayed. The upper level contains the bedrooms and baths, the most unique of which has gold fixtures and pink tile. In later years, Bradley was confined to a wheelchair and spent most of his hours on the lower level of the house, gazing out at the view which he had created.

Col. Bradley was responsible for erecting most of the barns and other buildings on the farm, all of which are painted white with green trim. During his stewardship, all employees lived on the farm and were either Irish Catholic or African-American. The farm was almost completely self-sufficient with gardens, a wash house, a school, a chapel, and a boarding house for bachelor workers.

Photographs of Col. Bradley show an unsmiling man, who seems stern and forbidding. On the contrary, however, he was a humanitarian and philanthropist. In Florida, he donated Beach Club profits to help build a church, later named St. Edwards in his honor. He supported many of Kentucky's orphanages, donating and raising thousands of dollars each year. Col. Bradley was also generous with his employees and would often continue paying his employees after they became too old to work. If an employee died, he would remain on the payroll as long as any of his dependents lived.

In 1946, at the age of 87, Col. Bradley died and Idle Hour Farm was sold and divided. Eleven years later, John Galbreath of Columbus, Ohio, bought the nucleus of the original farm and renamed it Darby Dan Farm. Like Col. Bradley, John Galbreath was a self-made man, who began working at the age of eight selling homemade horseradish. He was the confidante of world leaders and at ease with the Queen of England, who has visited the farm. According to the farm's former business manager, Pam Michul, John Galbreath was a generous man, who treated everyone, from stable hand to Queen, with the same amount of respect. He was also the patriarch of a loving and close-knit family. As the main house had sat vacant for more than a decade after Col. Bradley's death, it had badly deteriorated; however, the seven grandchildren took an interest in the house, restoring it in time for Queen Elizabeth's October 1984 visit.

John Galbreath was also a sports enthusiast. For forty years, he owned, loved, and won with both the Pittsburgh Pirates baseball team and his Thoroughbred horses. He won the English Derby once (with Roberto, 1972, named for Roberto Clemento of the Pirates), the Kentucky Derby twice (Chateaugay, 1963, and Proud Clarion, 1967), and the World Series three times. His foundation sire, Ribot, an Italian import, won the Prix de l'Arc de Triomphe twice and was unbeaten in 16 races, and in 1985, he won the Breeders' Cup with Proud Truth.

In August 1988, at the age of 90, John Galbreath died, and the farm has since transitioned from a private operation to a commercial facility. Now under the management of partners John Phillips and T. Wayne Sweezey, the farm offers a full range of services, including boarding and sales preparation. Its stallion operation includes bloodlines from such equine giants as A. P. Indy (Suave), Unbridled (Saarland), and Mr. Prospector (Aldebaran). With its exceptional past and forward thinking vision, Darby Dan is a unique farm that is committed to its motto: Devoted to the horse. Dedicated to our clients. ✒

*Generally, a horse can be named whatever its owner desires, with some exceptions:*

> *(1) The name cannot sound like or look like a name used by a horse until ten years have past after that horse's death (a gelding's name can be used five years after its death) as no two horses should be at a track with the same name.*

> *(2) If the owner has a sire or dam with an exceptional record, he will usually try to incorporate the name in some manner into the name given to the foal. In no event, however, can a name that has become famous such as Secretariat or Man o' War be reused.*

*The owner must submit a list of six possible names to The Jockey Club, who will run the choices through its computer to ensure there are no violations of these rules. Many names are chosen strictly by whimsy as in genetically-engineered Thoroughbred colt Blarney Colt, who was sired by Irish Castle out of Jeanne Splicer; Thoroughbred Bates Motel who sired the filly, Last Shower; and Northern Dancer, who sired Nureyev and Nijinsky II. And, then there's God Knows Who, who won at Santa Anita on April Fool's Day in 1988.*

# Darley at Jonabell

Clearly one of the most prestigious farms in the Bluegrass region, Darley at Jonabell was operated for many years as Jonabell Farm by members of the John A. Bell III family. Mr. and Mrs. John A. Bell III originally operated the much smaller Jonabell on land leased from Hamburg Place, beginning in 1946. Bell purchased the core of the farm at its present location on Bowman Mill Road in 1954. This farm grew to include 800 acres and remained under the Bell family's control until 2001,

when it was sold to Sheikh Mohammed bin Rashid al Maktoum, and it became part of his extensive Darley operation.

The farm's main house, known as the Abraham Bowman house, is listed on the National Register of Historic Places. This two-story, five-bay brick house was built in the early 1800's, and a one-story, three-bay front porch was a later addition. Downstairs, the woodwork is predominantly walnut and the floors are ash. Elaborately-designed molding frames the door and window openings, and beautiful mantels are mounted over the large fireplaces. Located to the right of the residence is a hand-chipped stone water tower, believed to have been built in the early 1900's by railroad executive Ed Corrigan, also former owner of the Hawthorne Race Track in Chicago.

Darley at Jonabell boasts a rich equine heritage, as the farm has produced over 200 stakes horses and 14 champions. It has housed such notable stallions as Triple Crown winner Affirmed, who was moved to Jonabell from Calumet Farm in August 1991. One of only eleven - and as of 2007 the last U.S. Triple Crown winner - Affirmed was a champion every year he raced (at 2, 3, and 4), won 14 Grade 1 races and was twice Horse of the Year. Upon his retirement, Affirmed was syndicated for $14.4 million, a record at the time. He has sired some 80 stakes winners and was elected to the National Museum of Racing and Hall of Fame. Affirmed died in January 2001 and is buried on the farm next to the stallion complex.

Many top horses have been raised at Jonabell, including Damascus, 1967 Horse of the Year and a leading sire; Epitome, champion 2-year-old filly and Breeders' Cup winner; Summing and Highland Blade, winner and runner-up in the 1981 Belmont Stakes; and Opening Verse, who won the 1990 Breeders' Cup Mile as well as over $1.6 million. In 2001, Jonabell stallion and 1994 Horse of the Year Holy Bull, was inducted into the Racing Hall of Fame.

Current owner Sheik Mohammed bin Rashid al-Maktoum, ruler of Dubai, appears to share his love for his country with his passion for horses, having been the leading buyer at the September yearling sales for many years. He now employs over 160 people to manage some of the area's finest horses and some of its largest acreage. After his brother's death in 2006, Gainsborough Farm was merged with Jonabell to create Darley America. The merger brought the combined acreage to over 4,000.

Darley at Jonabell serves as the stallion division of Darley America. For the 2007-2008 breeding season, stallions include sires of Kentucky Derby winners: Holy Bull, sire of Giacomo; Street Cry, sire of Street Sense; Elusive Quality, sire of Smarty Jones; and Quiet American, sire of Real Quiet. Other stallions include 2006 Champion 3-year-old Bernardini, 2007 Kentucky Derby Winner Street Sense, Champion Cherokee Run, sire of 2007 Breeders' Cup Juvenile winner War Pass, as well as young Grade 1 winners Hard Spun, Discreet Cat and Any Given Saturday. 🖋

*Handchipped Water Tower*

*Darley at Jonabell*
3333 Bowman Mill Rd
Lexington, KY 40513
(859) 255-8537

# Dixiana Farm

*The sign on the gate read:*

Nothing Except A Good **RACE HORSE** Wanted
\*\*\*\*\*
Agents For the Sale of Books, Patent Medicines,
Sewing Machines, Agricultural Implements,
Horticulture & Nursery Products and
**ESPECIALLY**
Of Lightning Rods And Wire Fences
**NOT ADMITTED**
\*\*\*\*\*
**VISITORS**
Of Every Nationality
Who Will Come Unto My House
**ALWAYS WELCOME**

\*\*\*\*\*

B. G. Thomas[2]

With that warning—and welcome—Major Barek G. Thomas set the tone for Dixiana Farm. Major Thomas, a typical Southern gentleman and one of the first professional horsemen in the area, was also a bachelor who kept an open house, and his hospitality to friends and fellow horsemen was legend.

Major Thomas graduated from Indiana University and received a law degree from Transylvania University in 1849. After practicing law for several years, he became a civil engineer for the Lexington & Frankfort Railroad, later serving as their agent in Lexington. Unfortunately, in 1861, while Lexington was occupied by Union troops, he shot and wounded a Union soldier involved in a disturbance outside the railroad station and hurriedly left town. He enlisted in the Confederate Army and rose to the rank of major before his discharge in

1865. When he returned to Lexington, he found that with the exception of a six-year-old filly named Dixie, most of his assets had been sold to pay his outstanding debts. Although steady jobs were hard to come by, the Major's brother, Charles, was circuit judge and appointed him Fayette County's Master Commissioner, a post which he held until his brother's death in 1873. He then served two terms as sheriff, retiring at the age of 50 to devote his full attention to his Thoroughbred breeding and racing operation.

In 1877 Thomas purchased 250 acres on Elkhorn Creek and named it Dixiana for his favorite mare. Dixie. From the late 1870's through 1891, he produced some of America's most famous horses, including Herzog, Ban Fax, Correction, and Hira, dam of Himyar. Himyar and Mannie Gray produced the horse for which Dixiana was best known—the "black whirlwind," Domino, the only colt to be the top money winner in his first year of racing.

With more outstanding debts than cash, in 1891 Thomas was forced to sell Dixiana. Two years later the farm was again sold, this time to Major Thomas J. Carson, of Natchez, Mississippi, a breeder of Thoroughbred horses and game chickens and an accomplished duelist. Carson was soon challenged to a duel and slightly wounded his opponent. Dueling was illegal in Kentucky and the major was arrested. At trial, he was assessed a hefty fine, which he refused to pay, insisting he'd rather spend time in jail. This seems to have been a good move, since the jail soon became the center of Lexington's social scene. Elaborately-prepared meals, complete with drinks, were delivered from the kitchen of the Phoenix Hotel, and card games with friends were daily events. (One of Carson's friends was

August Belmont, founder of Belmont Park. Carson gave him the sign which had been at Dixiana's gates, and it was hung at Belmont Park.)

Carson died in the early 1900's, and the farm became a part of James Haggin's Elmendorf Farm. Upon Haggin's death, it was sold to O. O. Carpenter, and in 1925 it was sold to J. C. Brady. Brady added 750 acres and completely renovated the entire farm, including the main house.

No one knows exactly when this house was built, but it is known

## Dixiana Farm
1301 Dixiana Domino Road
Lexington, KY 40511
(859) 299-1223

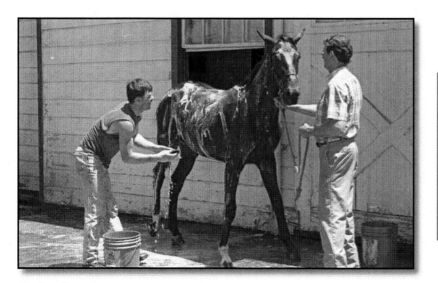

*Yearling Grooming*

*A horse farm with plank fences will almost always have paddocks with rounded corners because a horse that runs into a square corner, can hit the fence, and inflict a severe, if not fatal, injury.*

that it was standing as early as 1861 and possibly even before. It has been extensively redecorated with random-width oak floors throughout. The living room is a combination of white-painted and dark-paneled pine walls and has an exposed beam ceiling. A large working fireplace is the focal point of the room. A door off this room leads to the cellar where there is a hidden door, behind which is a false wall which is believed to be the entrance to a tunnel which exits next to Elkhorn Creek some 100 yards away. (Although no one knows exactly what the purpose of this tunnel was, some say that Dixiana was once a part of the underground railroad system, and that this tunnel was a passageway for escaping slaves. Another supposition is that the tunnel was to be used in the event of an Indian attack.)

*Horse Admiring Jockey*

In addition to renovating the house, Brady also planted hundreds of trees, built miles of fences, erected several barns and built a stone bridge over the creek. Brady died before completing his planned renovations, and in 1928 the entire farm was sold to Charles Fisher (of Body by Fisher), who bought the original 250 acres and three additional farms as well, one of which was Domino Stud, raising Dixiana's total acreage to 800.

After Fisher bought Dixiana, the farm became known for show horses such as Beau Wolf, who won the five-gaited championship at the International Livestock Exposition in the early 1930's, Kings Genius, and Belle Royal. It was also the home of such outstanding Thoroughbreds as Mata Hari, an exceptional runner and broodmare, and Sweep All, who ran second in the 1931 Kentucky Derby and sired many stakes winners. In June 1947, Fisher sold the Dixiana saddle horses and much of the farm's acreage, keeping the original 250 plus an additional 105 acres. After his death, his daughter, Mary, remained on the farm until it was sold to Dixiana Farms, Inc., who sold it to its present owner, William Shively, in 2004. Shively completely renovated most of the barns and now keeps a racing stable as well as a broodmare operation. 🖎

*Bridge at Dixiana*

# Domino Stud

## Domino Stud

3744 Russell Cave Road
Lexington, KY
(859) 293-1436.
www.dominostud.com

Domino Stud features traditional white plank fence, large paddocks and pastures, and green and white outbuildings. The land on which Domino now sits was originally in two tracts; one owned by Joseph Harrison (son of Elk Hill Farm's Robert Harrison) and the other by William Russell, Jr., of Mt. Brilliant Farm. In the mid-1800's, however, these two tracts were combined to make Domino, which was then given to William Grant Moore by his parents.

Domino changed owners many times over the years, once becoming part of Elmendorf Farm and then a part of Dixiana. In 1971 the farm was bought by Coca-Cola entrepreneur W. B. Terry, who made many improvements to the farm, including restoration of the main house. Built by Moore in 1832, the house is constructed of bricks made from clay found on the farm, and the

planks in the floor came from the farm's trees. The front of the house is believed to have been added in 1846 by local architect John McMurtry. Terry added 6,000 square feet which expanded the three-story, Greek Revival style house to its present 23,000 square feet. The main house has a shake roof, a sheltered entrance court, a landscaped brick walkway, and is furnished with fine antiques. Exceptionally striking is the glass-enclosed 1,856 square foot garden room with its Vermont marble floor.

The story of Domino Stud today, however, is the story of its current owner, Kenneth Thomas Jones, Jr., who bought the farm from Terry in August 1989. Jones wrote a check for Domino Stud for slightly more than $10,000,000, then the second highest price paid for a horse farm in Kentucky. At the same time, he also purchased Mt. Brilliant Farm which has since been sold.

A resident of Guam, Ken Jones was born on a tobacco farm in Willow Springs, North Carolina, a small country town just south of Raleigh. He claims that he acquired most of his knowledge of horseflesh from walking for so many years behind a plow horse. He left the farm when he was 18 and moved to Raleigh where he worked for the Department of Agriculture. An athletic man who enjoyed rodeo riding and boxing, he won the Golden Gloves Boxing Award during the mid-1930's. In Wake Forest, North Carolina, on his 21st birthday, Jones was appointed the youngest Chrysler dealer in the state. He successfully managed that dealership until 1942, when he was inducted into the Naval Construction Battalion of the U. S. Navy. He participated in the July 21, 1944 invasion of Guam which wrestled control of the island from the Japanese.

Jones recognized that there was a whole lot more going on in Guam than was necessary to fight a war. The United States was building streets, superhighways, and large airfields. He liked the area and believed that when the war ended, business opportunities would be plentiful.

Jones was stationed in Guam for a little more than a year. During that time, he and his partner, Segundo Guerrero, mapped out plans for a post-war business, and when Jones returned to North Carolina in 1945, he put those plans in action.

Because of an 11 pound limit on items being mailed into Guam, Jones knew that small objects would be the best merchandise for him to send back for resale. Deciding that jewelry would be a hot item in Guam, he bought up what was readily available in North Carolina and mailed it back to Guerrero, who had set up a small jewelry store on his front porch. Guerrero would sell the jewelry and send the money back to Jones, who would then buy the next shipment. This, according to Jones, went "very well."

In 1946 Jones returned to Guam as a civil service employee, a requirement for mainlanders wanting to stay on the island for any length of time. After six months, he went into business on a full-time basis. He married and had three daughters— Vivian, Linda and Ronnie—who are now living in the United States.

Much of Guam had been destroyed during the war, so Jones and Guerrero went into the construction business, obtaining reconstruction contracts to rebuild the area. They also built the Town House, which became the leading department store in Guam. They had the first supermarket, the first automobile agency, the first Kentucky Fried Chicken, and the first hotel on both Guam and Saipan. For 22 years, they had a cattle ranch and dairy farm that supplied fresh milk to Guam's school children. In time they acquired other businesses, including a shipping vessel for bringing goods back to Guam. In 1967 they became involved in the tourism business. At that time there were only some 5,000 visitors to Guam each year and many of those were there for business reasons only. Today there are approximately 750,000 visitors to the island each year, which Jones believes to be his main contribution to the area's economy.

Jones makes his business success sound easy, but it is obvious that he is an astute businessman, who doesn't mind and probably enjoys hard work. He is a modest person, very much a family man. He married his current wife, Elaine, also of Guam, in 1972 and they have two daughters, Ramona and Donna. Part of Jones's success can be attributed to the loyalty which he invokes in his employees, many of whom have been with him for more than 30 years. He inspires this loyalty with his thoughtfulness: when he purchased Domino Stud, he visited each of the farm's tenants to listen to their suggestions or complaints, to see that

their needs were being met, and that their housing was comfortable.

Jones has been involved in the horse business since 1960 and keeps racehorses in Australia, racing under the blue, yellow and black colors of Guam. Most of his horses race exclusively in Australia where the purses are on a par with those in the United States and where there are races almost every day of the week, with good tracks and excellent facilities. Jones won the Australian Oaks with India's Dream, and the Magic Millions Classic in January 1992, with Clan O'Sullivan. In April of '92, Clan O'Sullivan ran second in Australia's Golden Slipper and the following month won the million dollar Magic Millions Australasian Two-Year-Old Classic, pushing his earnings to almost

*Domino's Horse Cemetery*

$1,750,000. In February 1993, Jones won the Cadbury Australian Guineas with Kenny's Best Pal.

Even though Jones has been in the racing business since 1960, he maintains that a person isn't really in the horse business until he's in Kentucky in the horse business. As the story goes, Mrs. Jones was aware of his desire for a Kentucky farm, and while they were vacationing in San Francisco, she picked up a copy of *Estates* magazine where she saw an ad for Domino Stud. She showed him the ad and informed him that there was his Kentucky ranch. He called the realtor, made arrangements to see it, and bought it a few days later.

The farm has produced some of the country's leading Thoroughbreds—an early example being wonder horse Domino, who was foaled on the farm on May 4, 1891. Sold as a yearling to James R. Keene, Domino was the only horse to be the leading money winner in his first year. After only two years at stud, he produced twenty foals, eight of which were stakes winners. These included Cap and Bells, who won the 1901 Epsom Oaks, and champion Commando, who sired nine stakes winners, including the undefeated Colin and Peter Pan, winner of the 1907 Belmont. Domino died in July 1897. His epitaph, written by owner, James R. Keene, reads: "Here lies the fleetest of runners the American Turf has ever known, and one of the gamest and most generous of horses."

Another farm great was Grey Dawn II, sire of 68 stakes winners, whose winnings totaled more than $26,000,000. He was ranked among the leading sires in the country until his death at the age of 29. The farm now has approximately 30 broodmares and accepts boarders, its primary equine business now being located in Australia.

*A farrier is a person who shoes horses, and should not be confused with a blacksmith who works with iron in a forge and may or may not shoe horses. Farriers are not government-regulated, and no formal training is required. However, there are approximately 50 schools across the United States and Canada where the trade is taught. Most would-be farriers voluntarily attend some type of school and/or serve an apprenticeship, and the American Farriers Association sponsors seminars and conferences to provide training and the most up-to-date information to its members. Although there are no actual figures available, it is estimated that there are at least 30,000 farriers across the United States.*

*There are a number of reasons for putting shoes on a horse—to protect the feet, provide traction on the racetrack, and, in some cases, to help straighten a foal's legs. And, according to Kelly Werner of the American Farriers Association, there are as many different types of horse shoes as there are shoes for people. Some are "ready mades," and some are made by hand. Some are made of aluminum, some of steel. There may be differences in weight, shape, and traction. To shoe a horse on all four feet generally costs between $55 to $75, and may take an hour or so to complete. As a horse's feet never quit growing, the procedure must be repeated every four to six weeks, whether the shoes have worn out or not. As the outer sole of the hoof is not sensitive to pain, shoeing is not a painful procedure.*

# Elmendorf Farm

This great horse farm has been producing champions—and winning Derbies— since the 1870's. After Kentucky native James Ben Ali Haggin's purchase in 1897, Elmendorf became one of the biggest and most opulent farms in the Bluegrass region of Kentucky.

When Haggin acquired the 544-acre Elmendorf, he owned in excess of a million acres in the West. Accustomed to living life on a grand scale, he soon grew dissatisfied with his comparatively small Kentucky farm and began to add as much of the land around Elmendorf as was available. He was very successful: at the time of

*Elmendorf Farm*
3931 Paris Pike
Lexington, KY 40511
(859) 299-2000

his death in 1914, Elmendorf had grown to over 8,000 acres.

Haggin made many improvements to his expanding farm. He added an office, a gatehouse, and a waiting station. (At one time the Lexington trolley system had a sidetrack through Elmendorf. The waiting station was used by farm employees who rode the trolley to and from work.) Haggin also built some of the finest barns in Kentucky, including the 27-stall foaling barn, known as the "Stork Barn." This red-brick barn, easily recognized by the large, porcelain stork standing guard over the entrance, is so well-constructed that regardless of the weather, the water in the horses' buckets would not freeze. At the intersection of four farm roads, Haggin constructed the "Lions' Circle," where the Lexington Ball was held for many years, and for his new bride, he built the 40-room, million-dollar mansion, "Green Hills." Although flamboyant, Haggin was also practical, and Elmendorf soon became completely self-sufficient, with a greenhouse, water tower, vegetable gardens, cattle and other livestock. To move his cattle from the west side of the Paris Turnpike to the east (a trip that was risky even then), a tunnel large enough to accommodate a herd of cattle was dug under the road. (Although now sealed at both ends, the tunnel still runs beneath Paris Pike.) Tunnels were also dug from Green Hills to both the carriage house and the greenhouse so that Haggin and his family could get to these buildings in bad weather.

Over the years Haggin tried, without success, to buy the thousand acres owned by his neighbor, John T. Hughes. The rumor is that Hughes left his entire estate to his housekeeper, who was the mother of Hughes's son, with the admonition that she could do whatever she liked with his estate, except sell it to Elmendorf. However, through the shenanigans of an unscrupulous New York lawyer, she was tricked out of her legacy and her land was taken by Elmendorf.

The truth is at least as interesting as the rumor. John Hughes was 83 years old and unmarried when he died. Ellen Davis, once Hughes's mother's slave, was Hughes's "faithful servant." In November 1923, while throwing rocks at a turkey, Hughes fell and broke his hip. He was taken to the hospital where he lingered, ultimately dying some nine months later. Shortly after his accident, Hughes made his will. After making provisions for his and Ms. Davis's son, Robert Henry Hughes, he gave 273.5 acres from his home place, his house, and various other items to Davis, age 80 at the time. The remainder of the home place he left to a local orphanage. The will was contested, but on December 15, 1925, the Court ruled in Ms. Davis's favor. On February 26, 1926, Ms. Davis did sell her bequest, but sold it to Payne Whitney, who owned what is today a part of Gainesway Farm.

*Part of the Lion's Circle*

The acreage left to the orphanage, however, was sold to Elmendorf.

Haggin's estate was not completely settled until ten years after his death. In 1917, John Madden purchased a portion of the property; he later sold his interest to Joseph Widener who later added an additional 587 acres. Widener built several barns, two of which are located on what is now the Normandy Farm, and the other being the circular barn on Clovelly Farm. Widener owned Elmendorf during the Depression and the taxes on Green Hills were enormous. It is said that he offered to give the mansion to the state if the state would maintain it; however, the state refused, and the mansion was razed. Today only the steps, the four great columns, and the lion statuary remain as a testament to the Haggin era.

Widener built the second "main house" in the early 1900's, using dark oak, pegged paneling salvaged from Green Hills. Now an office, the three-story stone house has

*All that Remains of "Green Hills"*

*Elmendorf Trolley Station*

*Dinwiddie Lampton*

Sri Lanka, who kept the Elmendorf name. Under his direction, the farm became the nation's leading breeder of Thoroughbreds, and from 1971 through 1979 Elmendorf consistently ranked in the top ten in terms of money won. (Gluck also founded the Maxwell Gluck Equine Research Center located at the University of Kentucky, which is a world-renowned center for the advancement of equine medicine.) In 1989, the farm was sold to Washington Redskins owner, Jack Kent Cooke, of Middleburg, Virginia, and after Cooke's death eight years later, the farm was sold to Dinwiddie Lampton, president of American Life & Accident Insurance Company of Kentucky. Mr. Lampton purchased an additional 200 acres, and now leases out a total of 500 acres to a Thoroughbred operation, keeping the remaining 200 for Elmendorf.

Mr. Lampton, and his wife, Elizabeth, have invested much of their energy and assets in the restoration of the farm. Although an octogenarian, Mr. Lampton is actively involved in the management of his insurance business and in the restoration and maintenance of Elmendorf. All of the buildings have been re-roofed, and the wait station has been completely renovated.

Both of the Lamptons are accomplished drivers and trainers – he was the first inductee into the Culver Hall of Fame

oak parquet floors and marble fireplaces. In the newly-remodeled kitchen, there is evidence of a now-defunct dumbwaiter. As was the custom, the house was built so that servants could go from the basement (then the kitchen) to the third floor (servants' quarters) without entering the living area of the house. In 1927 a guest cottage, attached by a breezeway to the main house, was added.

After Widener's death in 1943, the farm passed to his son and then to his grandson, Peter A. B. Widener III, who divided the land and sold it. From the 1,287 acres came Normandy Farm, Clovelly Farm, and a portion of Spendthrift Farm. The remaining 504 acres were subsequently purchased by Maxwell Gluck, former ambassador to

*In the early 1600's, the coachmen of stylish English families began wearing the colors with which their particular family was most associated. Soon this practice was followed by English jockeys as well. To be more easily recognized, jockeys soon wore brightly colored caps and jackets with a combination of colors called silks for the material of which they are most often made. In the United States silks are registered with the Jockey Club.*

and she is Director of the American Hackney Horse Society Foundation. Mrs. Lampton's horse, Saint, was an honored guest at their wedding held at Elmendorf in 2004 – it was Saint who was responsible for their 1980 meeting when both were competing in Saratoga.

Over the years, many legendary horses have been produced at Elmendorf, including Ben Ali, Firenzi, Spendthrift, and Fair Play {Man o' War's sire and for three years the leading sire in North America). Under the Lamptons' direction, the farm is still producing winners, but the emphasis is now on carriages and the horses that pull them. The stork barn has been converted to a coach barn, where some of his antique carriages are displayed on floors covered with exquisite Oriental rugs. Although he is down to 100 carriages (from an estimated high of 300), the collection of vintage and antique carriages (which include sleighs, hackneys, landaus, phaetons, and even a stagecoach) is still impressive.

Although there is still a Jim, Ben, Ali, and Haggin on the farm, those names now refer to the Lamptons' carriage horses who were trained and driven by Elizabeth Lampton, with Mr. Lampton as passenger, at the 2007 Junior League horse show, the third largest show in the United States.. The Lamptons have hosted the Patron's Party Gala on behalf of the League for the past seven years. A trophy to be given annually for performance excellence in the Coaching Four-in-Hand Class has been established in Mr. Lampton's honor.

*The Lamptons at Horse Show*

*Although groups of mares and mares with foals may be kept together in large pastures, stallions, due to their aggressive natures, must be kept in separate paddocks. Thus, many farms have double fences between neighboring horses which not only separate the horses, but also provide an aisle through which a horse may be led without damage or disturbance to his neighbor. Also, a plank fence must be built behind a stone fence to protect a horse from cutting himself on the rough stone and to keep him from jumping over the much lower stone wall.*

# Gainesway Farm

Gainesway Farm has all the requisites for a traditional Bluegrass farm - spacious green paddocks, black plank fences, and ornately constructed barns - yet it is a thoroughly modern Thoroughbred farm, utilizing the most advanced equine farming technology. One of the largest stallion operations in the country, this winning combination of tradition and technology was developed by John R. Gaines, one of racing's most-honored patrons.

John's grandfather, Thomas, was the first in the Gaines family to become involved in the horse business. While operating a Standardbred nursery and Grand Circuit racing stable, he also sold chicken, cattle, and sheep feed in upstate New York. When John's father, Clarence, joined the company, the feed mill was expanded to include dog rations, and the Gaines Dog Food Company was born. The success of this business allowed the Gaines family to pursue their love of harness racing. In 1939 Clarence Gaines bought his first horse, Precise, a champion as both a two- and three-year-old, and subsequently established a Standardbred farm in Lexington, Kentucky, on the property where Gainesway Subdivision is now located.

John Gaines was introduced to trotters at an early age, and although he has been involved in all areas of the horse business, he was particularly interested in the breeding aspect. After graduating from Notre Dame, he studied genetics at the University of Kentucky. In the late 1950's, after John's father sold the original Lexington farm, John entered the trotting-horse business.

At the age of 28, Gaines bought his first farm and syndicated his first stallion, Demon Hanover, for a half-million dollars, harness racing's first stallion syndication. He later sold both the farm and his horses and leased the Keene farm on Versailles Road, where he combined his love of Standardbreds with his new interest in Thoroughbreds. In 1964 Gaines created the Thoroughbred division of Gainesway with the

*Stallion Complex Fountain*

acquisition of the filly Oil Royalty, who became a major stakes winner and champion, and the highly successful broodmare Cosmah. Five years later he bought 500 acres on the Paris Pike from C. V. Whitney and in the next twenty years built Gainesway Farm into an outstanding equine business.

Over time, Gaines constructed one of the world's most lavish stallion complexes. Built in 1981 at a cost of some $200,000 per barn, the complex includes eight, four-stall barns designed to provide the utmost in safety and comfort for its million-dollar residents. In front of the complex, there is a 170' water trough and a reflecting pool surrounded by a stone wall. The A-frame barns are separated by oak trees and joined by pathways of reddish-brown brick chips. The barns have high-pitched, inch-thick clay tile roofs, which provide excellent ventilation. Each stall has a wrought-iron door, and the two windows in each stall provide natural lighting, which is supplemented by skylights, window

*Gainesway Farm*
3750 Paris Pike
Lexington, KY 40511
(859) 293-2676
www.gainesway.com

*Garden Statue*

slots, and 9' doorways. The complex includes a huge exercise arena where horses can be broken as well as exercised, and a highly efficient breeding shed where two sessions can occur simultaneously.

John Gaines produced both champion trotters and champion runners. His trotters have won every major stakes race in America, and during the 1980's,

his stallions and their progeny earned over $525 million, a world's record. He supported the equine industry and his community in other ways as well: he helped develop the Kentucky Horse Park; helped create the Breeders' Cup classic; and founded the Gaines Center for the Humanities. For his service to the industry, in 1991 Gaines was guest of honor at the Thoroughbred Club of America's 60th Testimonial Dinner.

In 1989, Gaines sold the 500-acre Gainesway Farm to South African horseman Graham Beck, who also owns the adjoining, 600-acre Greentree Farm. In addition to these farms, both of which are operated under the Gainesway name, Beck leases 500 acres of the C. V. Whitney farm, giving him a total of 1,600 acres on Paris Pike, one of the Bluegrass region's more prestigious addresses. Beck, who made his fortune in the coal mines of Africa, also owns 295 acres on Old Frankfort Pike, 480 acres in Woodford County, and 4,000 acres in South Africa, where he is one of the country's top breeders and racers. He and his son, Antony, have continued the tradition of excellence at Gainesway.

Today, the farm boards and prepares and sells horses for others in Kentucky and New York. It also continues to stand some of the world's most famous stallions, including Afleet Alex, who had eight wins in twelve starts and a total earnings of $2,765,800; Mr. Greeley, whose progeny have earned over $34 million, (one of whom, Whywhywhy, now stands at Gainesway as well); and Cuvee, a grandson of Mr. Prospector.

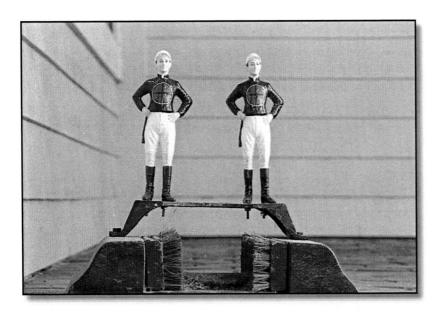

*Attention to Detail Reflected in Boot Scraper*

The 1789 census showed Lexington with a population of approximately 9,000 people and 9,607 horses.

# Hamburg Place

Hamburg Place is one of the more elegant Bluegrass farms. With its stone walls, black and red barns, and well-tended grounds, it is an uncommonly-beautiful farm, one of few in the area to be owned by the same family since its birth. At one time, it was also one of the area's largest farms, with 2,000 acres dedicated to the business of breeding and racing blooded horses.

Hamburg Place was developed as both a Thoroughbred and Standardbred farm by John E. Madden, known for three decades as "The Wizard of the Turf." Madden was born in 1856 in Bethlehem, Pennsylvania, to parents who had only recently immigrated from Ireland. His father, Patrick, died in 1860 and left his wife and three children almost penniless. John was gifted, however, with a fleet foot, alert mind, and a keen eye for

## Hamburg Place
2150 Paul Jones Way
Lexington, KY 40509
(859) 299-1515
www.hamburgplace.com

horses, assets which he parlayed into a multimillion-dollar estate. Appropriately enough, it was his athletic ability that bought and paid for his entry into the horse racing industry.

During the latter part of the 19th century, the county fair was at times the main event in small towns across the country, and it was there that John earned the money to buy his first horse. Moving from fair to fair, he competed in both foot and horse races. As he travelled, he would trade one horse for another, gradually improving his stock with each trade. When cash was needed, he would move on to other small towns where there was usually a local boxing or foot-racing champ with whom he could compete. Bets would be made and more often than not, John would win: by the time he was 28, he had a large enough herd of mediocre horses that he was able to trade for one good trotter.

From that unlikely beginning, John Madden worked his way to the top of the racing circuit. His philosophy was always, "Better to sell and repent than keep and repent." When he raced a horse, it was

with an eye on the potential market. If the horse became a great money winner after it was sold, then that was just good business. For example, Madden bought his first champion, Hamburg, as a weanling for $1,200, trained him, raced him (his earnings exceeded $38,000), and sold him as a champion for approximately $40,000. Four years later, Hamburg sold for $60,000 and after three more years, for $70,000.

In 1890 Madden married Anna Louise Megrue, and in 1891 they moved to Lexington. Settling into the Phoenix Hotel, John continued his pattern of "buying high and selling higher." In 1897 he purchased 235 acres on the Winchester Road for $30,000 and developed the farm which was to become Hamburg Place.

In less than 12 years, the farm had grown to 2,000 acres. For the exorbitant, then-record price of $75,000, an additional 80 acres were also bought. This land, however, had a large spring-fed pond which could provide both water for the farm and a swimming pool for John. When James Haggin died, Madden also bought the major part of Elmendorf land, paying for it by writing the first $1,000,000 check to clear a Lexington bank. This land was kept for only a few years and was sold at a profit to Joseph Widener.

At Hamburg, Madden owned and trained Plaudit, the 1898 Kentucky Derby winner. He bred five additional Derby winners, including Old Rosebud {1914), Sir Barton, who became the first Triple Crown winner in 1919, and Flying Ebony (1925). He was America's leading trainer twice (1901 and 1902), and his record as a breeder and owner is still outstanding

Before they were divorced in 1909, the Maddens had two children, John Edward, Jr., and Joseph. After a lengthy court dispute, John was granted custody of the boys. Although Edward moved back to the farm after his father's death in 1929, neither he nor his brother ever developed

Boot Scraper

an interest in the business that had been their father's passion. Grandson Preston, however, has followed in his famous grandfather's footsteps. Preston Madden took over the farm in 1956, and, less than 60 years after his grandfather's death, a Madden once again had bred the world's leading money-winning horse, Alysheba. In 1985 Alysheba sold for $500,000.

Preston Madden also bred Alysheba's little sister, Alysbelle, a major stakes winner at Santa Anita in 1992; owned T. V. Lark, who was champion grass horse in 1961, and who beat the mighty Kelso in the Washington, D. C. International before retiring to become the leading sire of 1974; and bred and owned Pink Pigeon, who set two world records at Santa Anita in 1968 (1-1/8 mile in 1:45 4/5) and 1969 (1-1/4 in 1:58 1/5).

For many years Preston and Anita Madden lived in the ivy-covered stone guest house that Jack Madden had used as lodging for polo playing guests. Preston doubled the size of the two-story cottage and put his office on the lower floor. In 1990 the Maddens moved to "Elmhurst," an antebellum mansion located on a 90-acre tract just across the road, and the guest house was converted to an office. Outside the office is a courtyard laid with bricks which once paved the streets of downtown Lexington. (When John Madden learned that the bricks were going to be removed, he sent a truck to pick them up and bring them back to Hamburg Place.)

There is a 16' x 16' stone tack room, also used as an office, and mile after mile of stone and black plank fences. The 100' black and red water tower located behind the office once provided water for the entire farm. All three generations of Maddens have planted trees such as sycamores, walnuts and hemlocks, and there are 200-year-old bur oaks on the farm as well. The barns, built by John Madden, are painted black and have red

*Sign on Barn Where Six Kentucky Derby Winners Were Foaled*

doors and trim. Throughout the farm are signs reminding visitors of the farm's main mission: "Drive Slowly. Horses Have the Right of Way."

Abutting Sir Barton Way in Lexington is the Hamburg Place Horse Cemetery, a distinctive graveyard where many of the farm's greatest are buried, the centerpiece of which is trotting great Nancy Hanks. Arranged in a horseshoe shape around her grave are Sir Barton, Derby winter Plaudit, leading sires Star Shoot and Ogden, and T. V. Lark and Pink Pigeon, among others. The Maddens have been restoring the cemetery and it is to be opened to the public when completed.

The house in which the Maddens now live was built in the late 1800's of building material found on the land. The stone was quarried on the site, the brick made from farm clay, and the logs were cut from farm trees. Originally built in the Victorian style, its former owners extensively remodeled the house in the early 1940's, creating a Greek Revival style mansion. The Maddens are still involved in the equine business, although stallions are no longer kept on the farm.

# Lane's End

### Lane's End

P. O. Box 626
Versailles, KY 40383
(850) 873-7300
www.lanesend.com

*Flower Box*

*L*ane's End, located in Woodford County, Kentucky, is one of the area's most prestigious Thoroughbred farms, and is recognized as the home of some of racing's most famous Thoroughbreds. Utilizing a blend of traditional design and modern equine management techniques, the owners, Mr. and Mrs. William S. Farish, designed the farm to be both practical and aesthetically pleasing.

Will Farish was born in Houston, Texas about 175 miles from the Lazy F Ranch owned by his family. As a result, Farish has been a horseman all his life and was an accomplished six-goal polo player.

In 1979, Farish purchased 1,500 acres of prime land in Central Kentucky, and began to develop Lane's End. The farm now consists of a total of some 2,000 acres, a portion of which was once the Bosque Bonita Farm, home to the dam of the great runner and sire Domino. Since that time additional property on Old Frankfort Pike was purchased, which became known as the Fort Blackburn Division. In 2004 more acreage on Midway Road was purchased, which is being renovated.

The farm's main house, designed by its first owner, Daniel Jackson Williams, was built in 1829. Called Pleasant Lawn, the 1-1/2 story brick house resembles two houses built back to back, connected by porticos with 21 columns. The house is only one room deep, with a front arcade of almost 50'.

Lane's End reflects the horsemanship, sophistication and quiet good taste of its owners. The barns are a traditional design, and each is a rich cream color. There is a beautifully-designed stallion complex consisting of three individual barns and a separate breeding shed. A courtyard for

showing the stallions has been added, and
the main stallion barn houses a viewing
room with DVD's of the stallions and their
progeny. Each of the barns has a splendid oak
interior, a cathedral ceiling, and eight 15' x
15' stalls. There are three yearling barns and
a landscaped show ring, which is decorated
with flowers from the farm's greenhouse.
There are four barns for the farm's hundred
or so broodmares, including a foaling barn
with rubberized floors and walls. Stalls in all
of the barns are extremely well-ventilated
and the floors are brick set in sand.

It is obvious that a great deal of care and
planning went into the development of the
farm. Fields were sown in bluegrass, and
hundreds of trees such as pear, oak, sweet
gum, and pine were planted. Almost 30
miles of black plank fence was built using
a topographic map to ensure that the fence
followed the natural contours of the land. As
the health and safety of the horses are the
first consideration at Lane's End, the fence
was built without corners and fence posts
were placed on the outside of the paddocks.

The individual stallion paddocks are

*Garden Statue*

large and are home to some of the finest stallions in the world. A. P. Indy, who was born and raised on the farm, won more than $2.9 million at the track and captured the Belmont Stakes and the $3 million Breeders' Cup Classic to be named the 1992 Horse of the Year. He has been the leading sire in North America on two separate occasions and is leaving a legacy not only through his own progeny but as a sire of sires and as a broodmare sire.

His half-brother Summer Squall, also won one of racing's Triple Crown events, the Preakness Stakes, and earned more than $1.8 million. A top stallion himself, Summer Squall sired Horse of the Year and Kentucky Derby winner Charismatic, another Lane's End

homebred. Summer Squall has retired from stud duty and still resides on the farm.

Currently the farm roster has 22 stallions, including five of the top 17 stallions standing in North America. Number one on the current list is Smart Strike with A.P. Indy holding the number two spot.

Lane's End employs approximately 100 people, and participates in a learning program that allows international students to work in and learn the Thoroughbred business. The Farish family wholeheartedly supports the Thoroughbred industry with contributions of both time and money.

Mr. Farish served as Chairman of the Board of Churchill Downs from 1992 to 2001, is a Steward and Vice Chairman of The Jockey Club, a Director of the Breeders' Cup and a trustee and member of the Board of Directors of the Keeneland Association. In addition, he has twice won the Eclipse Award for outstanding breeder.

Lane's End is a full-service Thoroughbred farm which provides boarding, breaking, breeding, and racing facilities. Farish and partners have bred more than 250 stakes winners and have been the leading consignors at the Keeneland sales many times. 🐦

*Statue of Dixieland Band*

# Overbrook Farm

$\mathcal{I}$n 1971, after a successful business career, William T. Young and his wife, Lucy, purchased a 110-acre farm on Delong Road near Lexington. The property, which had laid fallow for many years, included a rustic cottage in disrepair which the Youngs proceeded to restore. Over a period of 20 years, Mr. Young added a number of parcels to the original farm including a dairy farm named Overbrook, the name of the farm today which includes more than 2,300 acres.

A native of Lexington and exposed to friends in the horse business over the years, Young decided to get into the thoroughbred business. Although he had no background in the horse business, Mr. Young sought advice from a number of friends and industry experts. Among the first horses that Mr. Young purchased was the race mare Terlingua who subsequently produced Storm Cat who

## Overbrook Farm
2525 Delong Road
Lexington, KY 40588
(859) 273-1514

*Covered Bridge*

in construction to the restored cottage, has a concrete shingle roof, as do structures in the stallion complex, offering both fire protection and a long life.

Having graduated from the University of Kentucky with high distinction in 1939 and serving a stint in the Army, Mr. Young founded W. T. Young Foods, Inc. which manufactured Big Top peanut butter, the brand that eventually became Jif after being sold to Procter and Gamble. After selling this business, he founded the W. T. Young Storage Company. Until his death in 2004, he was clearly a part of the community in which he lived. He was involved in many civic and philanthropic causes, including the preservation of Shakertown and Transylvania University whose board he chaired for 22 years. In 1994, he contributed $5 million to the University of Kentucky for the construction of a new library, which now bears his name.

Mr. Young passed away in 2004, and the farm is now managed by his son, Bill Young, Jr. and daughter, Lucy Young Hamilton, as well as his grandson, Chris Young, who is the farm's racing manager. Current Overbrook stallions include Jump Start, Tactical Cat, Pioneering, and the legendary sire Storm Cat, who has sired 150 stakes winners and progeny with earnings of more than $103 million through 2006. Other active Overbrook stallions include 1999 Breeders' Cup Classic champion Cat Thief and 1996 Kentucky Derby winner Grindstone. The farm's broodmares number around 80.

became Overbrook's signature horse and one of the most successful stallions of the past thirty years. Today, Overbrook breeds, races, stands stallions and buys and sells horses. Through 2007, the farm had bred 109 stakes winners. In 1996, a homebred Grindstone won the Kentucky Derby, and Editor's Note won the Belmont - a rare double. In addition, Overbrook bred and campaigned champions Boston Harbor, Flanders, Golden Attraction and Surfside, as well as Cat Thief who won the Breeders' Cup Classic in 1999.

Overbrook Farm today is the result of Mr. Young's keen eye and vision. He was closely involved in the layout of pastures, fences and roads as well as the design and location of barns and other structures. Roads were located along ridges to provide scenic views; Kentucky limestone bridges were built over the creek, and miles of wooden fencing were installed to follow the contours of the land. Thousands of trees were planted, including the pine trees which border much of the farm. In addition to the brick mare barn whose cupola is the farm's symbol, a limestone barn, other masonry barns as well as wooden barns were constructed. All barns are well ventilated with outside doors for each stall. The farm office, which is similar

*The height of a horse is measured in* hands, *starting from the ground up to the withers (the ridge between the shoulder blades). Each hand equals 4" which is the average width of a man's hand.*

# Spendthrift Farm

*Spendthrift Farm*
884 Ironworks Pike
Lexington, KY 40511
(859) 294-0030
www.spendthriftfarm.com

*H*istoric Spendthrift Farm was created and managed by a man whose family had been a major power in the Thoroughbred business for several generations. Continuing that tradition, Leslie Combs II parlayed a modest 127 acres into almost 6,000 acres of prime Bluegrass land, on which were raised some of the most legendary racehorses that the sport has ever seen.

The original acreage, on which the "main house" was located, was purchased by Combs in 1937, having been carved out of a 900-acre estate known as Cherry Grove, then owned by Hector Lewis. Combs named the farm "Spendthrift," after the great stallion that had belonged to his great-grandfather, Daniel Swigert. (The horse, a Belmont Stakes winner, was the sire of Hastings, who sired Fair

*Nashua, A Champion*

Play, sire of Man 'o War.) The house, which had been built in 1804, became the core of the Combs's family home, which was enlarged and modernized over the years. Combs also gradually added acreage to the farm, purchasing tracts from his neighbors, renowned horsemen J. B. Haggin and George and Peter Widener.

As the farm grew in size, Spendthrift also grew in name recognition, soon becoming one of the most successful breeders and consignors in the business, ultimately breeding 107 stakes winners. Spendthrift stood eight Derby winners, as well as Preakness and Belmont winner Nashua. The farm was also known for its lavish parties, for many years hosting The Lexington Ball, which was, for many, the social event of the season. Attended by movie stars, debutantes, sports heroes, and

royalty, the event brought in hundreds of thousands of dollars for local charities.

Combs is credited with being the first to syndicate a stallion (in 1947). He was a founder of the Breeders' Sales Company, and the head of a syndicate which bought the first million-dollar horse, Nashua, in 1955. The farm also became one of the first to be traded publically, an unfortunate experiment that - coupled with the plunge of the Thoroughbred market in the late 1980s and early 1990s - led to the farm's bankruptcy. In 1994, Ted Taylor purchased the main 496-acre tract of Spendthrift at a court-ordered bankruptcy auction, for $5,250 an acre, and six years later it was sold to a partnership headed by horseman Bruce Kline.

The farm, now consisting of 733 acres, was resold in 2004 to B. Wayne Hughes, a California resident and founder of Public

*Jockey*

Storage, who was introduced to horse racing by his father. From a modest beginning as a horse owner, Hughes's success grew, and in 2003, his horse Action This Day, won the Breeders' Cup Juvenile at Santa Anita, later being named champion 2-year-old colt.

Hughes and his staff have preserved what they could of the once magnificent showplace, and have recreated what couldn't be salvaged. The house, now used as the farm's office, was extensively remodeled in 2007 and is being restored to its former majesty. Two of the twelve green and white barns had deteriorated to the point that they had to be replaced, as did much of the fencing. According to farm manager Ned Toffey, Hughes walks the line between preserving the history and feel of the farm, while maintaining good, solid practices to ensure the health and safety of the horses.

Hughes plans to continue to breed and produce stallions. Currently standing at Spendthrift is Action This Day, multiple graded stakes winner Don't Get Mad, and grade II stakes winner Teton Forest.

*On August 5, 1990, it was announced that a computer at the Laurel Race Course had determined once and for all the greatest race horse of the century. Pitting the 11 best horses against each other, the computer decided the "Ultimate Challenge Sweepstakes" would be won in the following order:* Kelso *(7-1 odds), by a neck, followed by* Man o' War *(3-1 odds), with* Secretariat *(the 5-2 favorite) coming in third. "Also rans finished as follows:* Citation, Spectacular Bid, Dr. Fager, Seattle Slew, Affirmed, Ruffian, Native Dancer, *and* Forego. *The 1-1/4 mile was raced in a record 1:59.*

*However, on December 11, 1991, the Hawthorne Race Course announced that* their *computer had pitted 26 of the best horses of the century against each other and that the winner of the simulated race was* Secretariat, *followed by* Man o' War, *and then* Kelso. *The rest of the field finished as follows:* Citation, Spectacular Bid, Forego, Swaps, Count Fleet, Native Dancer, Ruffian, Dr. Fager *and* Colin. *From this it can be determined that at least two computers agree on the top three horses of the century.*

# Stonestreet Farm

*Stallion Barn*

## Stonestreet Farm

3530 Old Frankfort Pike
Lexington, KY 40510

Although lacking the history and tradition of many farms, Stonestreet Farm is, in every sense, a horse-industry classic. Originally a modest cattle operation, this 469-acre farm was transformed into a showplace which combined the advantages of modern living with the beauty of the traditional Bluegrass farm.

The farm, then known as Buckram Oak, was purchased in January 1979 by Sheik Mahmoud Fustok and his family, who intended to make this farm the foundation for the family's international Thoroughbred operation. In two years—and at a reputed cost of several million dollars—the Fustoks had transformed the farm into a spectacular broodmare operation.

Six comfortable houses for farm workers were built, as well as a main house, guest house and tennis court enjoyed by the Fustok family and their guests. After the renovation ended, the only building left in its original condition was the red-brick, ranch-style house where the farm's general manager lived. The main house overlooks a large, five-acre lake which is spanned by two lovely arched bridges that are faced with Kentucky River limestone.

The five spacious, 20-stall barns have slate roofs with ornate cupolas and side dormers, and each has a gold-veneered weathervane. The interiors are paneled in red oak with stainless steel hardware, and the stalls are large and roomy. The barns are similar in both color and design to the buildings at the Kentucky Horse Park.

In the spring, thousands of narcissus bloom around the lake and on the lake's one-acre island. Three thousand new trees, the majority of which are oak, were planted along the 6-1/2 miles of blacktop road. In 1986, the Kentucky Chapter, American Society of Landscape Architects, presented the firm of Scruggs and Hammonds, Landscape Architects, with its Design Award in recognition of the farm's landscaping.

*Arched Bridge with Decorative Lighting*

Prior to his death in February 2006, Fustok sold Buckram Oak to Jess Stonestreet Jackson, founder of Kendall-Jackson Wine Estates, for 17.5 million. After renaming the farm in honor of his ancestors, Jackson began the process of hiring a new staff and moving his mares and foals to their new location. A few months later, he also purchased 640 acres of Adena Springs farm near Versailles, Kentucky. Although new to the area, Mr. Jackson appears to have moved in ready to go to work. He is a member of the Sales Integrity Task Force committee, and has been adding both land and horses to his already vast holdings. By mid-2005 he had over 150 mares on the farm, and 30 more on the track. The farm also has an interest in Curlin, who had won more than $2.4 million by August 2007 and is a contender for the Breeder's Cup.

Jackson comes from a long line of horse lovers and became involved in the Thoroughbred business for a short while in the early 1960's. In addition to his interest in Kendall-Jackson, he's also been a successful attorney, real estate investor, and computer entrepreneur.

*Gold-veneered Weathervane*

# Three Chimneys

## Three Chimneys

1981 Old Frankfort Pike
Versailles, KY 40383
(859) 873-7053
www.threechimneys.com

Three Chimneys' trademark is The Idea of Excellence, but it's apparent that this logo is more than just a slogan. Evidence of excellence is everywhere—from the well-manicured grounds to the newly-painted barns. According to director and former farm president Dan Rosenberg (who was named Executive in Residence for the Equine Initiative within the University of Kentucky College of Agriculture in 2006), Three Chimneys' long-range goal is to breed the best horses in the world. An ambitious goal, but with people like Rosenberg and farm owner Robert Clay managing the activities of the farm, it is proving to be within the realm of probability.

When he started out, Robert Clay knew little about the Thoroughbred business. What he knew of the practical side, he learned working in the barns at Spendthrift Farm, while a student at the University of Kentucky. What he knew of the business side, he learned when he wrote a paper on the subject at Harvard Business School. In 1972, however, Robert Clay and his wife began building Three Chimneys Farm. Ten years later, it was recognized as one of the country's finest horse breeding and boarding operations.

For practical reasons, Three Chimneys has been divided into

six separate divisions—five in Woodford County and one in Fayette County. This was a novel practice in the Bluegrass area, but Clay believes that a large farm is not always able to provide each horse with the individual attention it needs. Each division cares for 50 to 60 horses, and each has a farm manager who must be completely familiar with each horse.

To keep their horses both physically and mentally fit, each stallion at Three Chimneys has a two-acre paddock and is ridden daily. Rosenberg believes that horses are bred to be athletes, and that they run for the sheer joy of running. He maintains that horses have a strong sense of rivalry and race each other to establish a pecking order; that they know exactly what a race is all about, and that a good horse wants to win, desire being as important as ability.

The broodmare division is on the north side of Old Frankfort Pike, across the road from the farm office. On this tract is a log cabin, built in the late 1700's, which was purchased in Jessamine County, Kentucky, disassembled, moved to Three Chimneys, and reassembled. It was first used as an office and later became a guest house. There is a small lake just in front of the cabin, and a park bench has been placed near the lake so that guests can enjoy the view. Down the road is a giant silo, left as a reminder of what the farm had once been. The main house, built in the federal style, is also located on this tract. Three Chimneys' office and the Stallion Division are located on the south side of Old Frankfort Pike. Housed in what was once a farm residence, the office has been painted the farm colors of cream with green trim and has been extensively renovated and enlarged,

*Stallion Barn*

with polished hardwood floors, broad exposed timber beams, and open fireplaces.

Three Chimneys is primarily a breeding operation, with its stallion barn located just behind the office. Stalls in the front section of this barn are arranged in a circular pattern so that each stallion can see and hear the other. This section is topped by a glass cupola rising almost 50', which provides soft, natural lighting. The rear section houses the breeding area so that a stallion has to travel only a short distance for breeding. The farm has been home to some of racing's megastars, including Triple Crown winner Seattle Slew and his sons Slew o' Gold and Capote; Kentucky Derby winner Silver Charm; and Genuine Risk, the only filly to run in all three Triple Crown races. Currently, stallions standing at Three Chimneys include such greats as Smarty Jones, undefeated Kentucky Derby winner; Dynaformer, sire of 2006 Kentucky Derby winner Barbaro, and Rahy, sire of 75 stakes winners.

As a testament to the care which Three Chimneys bestows upon its horses, in the summer of 2007 - on record as one of the hottest seen in Kentucky - the long-retired 27-year-old Slew o' Gold was becoming seriously overheated. Suffering from Cushing's disease which makes it hard for him to regulate his body temperature, the two-time Eclipse Award winner was in serious trouble, although every effort was being made to lower the temperature of his overheated body. Standard treatments, however, weren't working, and it was becoming difficult for the old stallion to breathe. In a last ditch effort, the farm wrapped his stall in plastic and installed two air conditioners, which proved to be successful. All this for a horse that had been put to pasture more than five years ago.

*Guest House*

# Walmac International

Walmac International has been home to some of Thoroughbred racing's most outstanding superstars. Although a traditional Bluegrass showplace with black plank fence and well-tended grounds, it is a thoroughly modern farm, with a highly-prized stable.

Walmac, originally known as the Valley Farm, was part of a 2,000-acre tract granted in the 1700's to Joseph Beckley of Virginia. The portion which became Walmac was deeded to Clifton Thomson, who built the farm's main house, and when he died, W. Z. Thomson inherited the property. The farm was once part of Elmendorf Farm, but in 1936 it was sold to Robert Wallace McIlvain, who laid the foundation for the present Thoroughbred operation.

McIlvain was born in Michigan and raised in the west. He launched his career in the oil fields of Texas and Louisiana, working his way up the ladder until he became Vice President of Pure Oil Company. He was an avid polo player and racer of Standardbreds. He bought the Paris Pike property when his interest shifted to Thoroughbreds, and hired horseman Leslie Combs II as the farm's first manager. Under his direction, the farm prospered, breeding six $100,000 winners, including stakes winner Olney. It was not until McIlvain's death at the age of 84, however, that the farm produced its first champion, Royal Native, who was sold as part of McIlvain's estate.

Walmac was leased by a succession of businessmen and partnerships until the mid-1980's when it was bought by John T.

*Cowboy Memorabilia in Jones's Office*

L. Jones, Jr., a former member of one of those partnerships. Jones, born in Quanah, Texas, began his equine career working with the quarter horses raised on his family's farm. After his father's death, he worked as a trainer until he became interested in Thoroughbreds. He attended his first Central Kentucky yearling sale in 1965, and for the next 15 years or so, had a great deal of luck—both good and bad. After hitting a financial slump in the 60's, however, he worked his way back to the top, and under his leadership, Walmac became a major stallion producer.

Jones is a true cowboy: his office is furnished with collector saddles, spurs, bits, and bridles. The main house also reflects his Western heritage: under his direction it was completely redecorated and almost every room furnished in a Western motif, the walls are painted in earth tones and decorated with Western art and Indian artifacts. One of the more interesting rooms, however, is Jones' "cowboy" room. Hanging there are hundreds of spurs, bits, and bridles of all kinds and description. Mounted next to a massive mahogany bar is an imposing wooden steer's head, and a 3' sculpture of John Wayne sits on the bar. Chaps, branding irons, and arrowheads cover every available surface. A wood burning stove heats the room, and in the corner sits a beautiful - and functional - poker table.

Outside the house there are formal and informal flower beds, many designed by the farm's previous owners, who at one time employed three full-time gardeners. Behind the main house, there is a full-size greenhouse built to Mrs. McIlvain's specifications--considered state of the art both then and now—where orchids, ferns, houseplants, and

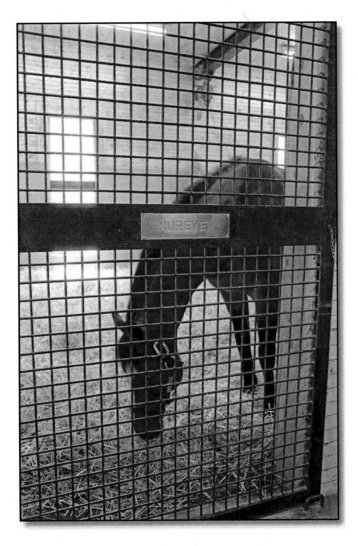

*Nureyev's Home*

red geraniums are grown. Geraniums, the farm's trademark flower, have been planted at various locations around the farm, and during horse sales, the farm's stable area is decorated with window boxes filled with their brilliant red blooms.

Walmac has stood such top sires as Alleged, whose offspring, Miss Alleged, won the 1991 Breeder's Cup Turf, and Miswaki, Mr. Prospector's leading son at stud. Miswaki sired 1993 Prix de l'Arc de Triomphe winner, Urban Sea, and Phone Trick, sire of Phone Chatter, winner of the 1993 Breeder's Cup Juvenile Fillies and an Eclipse award as champion two-year old filly. Perhaps best known however, is the great stallion, Nureyev.

During his breeding career, Nureyev sired 135 stakes winners and more than twenty champions. He was a remarkable horse, especially in light of the fact that in May 1987, he suffered an injury to his right hock from which he was given less than a 10% chance of survival. Had it not been for the farm's immediate intervention, there is little doubt that he would have had to have been destroyed; however, the farm spared no expense in saving his life. A team of surgeons operated almost immediately after the accident, and a special sling was designed to keep his weight off the injured leg. Within ten days after the accident, a small wooden barn had been constructed for his recuperation. Wayne Reinsmith, Nureyev's groom; J. D. Howard, Walmac's veterinarian and farm manager; and Kenneth Aubrey, the assistant farm manager, moved into the barn with Nureyev to oversee his recovery. These men and their patient fought setback after setback until December 1987 when he was judged fit to return to Walmac. There he was attended 24 hours-a-day and was hand-walked and hand-grazed. On April 1, 1988, he resumed stud duties, and, in spite of several prior fertility problems, in 1994 the farm could boast an 85% success rate. Nureyev died at age 24 on October 29, 2001, and is buried on the farm.

Although Jones sold Walmac in September 2004, to his son, John T. L. Jones, III, and his partner, Bobby Trussell, he remains involved as consultant and Director Emeritus. The farm remains dedicated to its stallion operation and stands such greats as Bandini, Songandaprayer, Sunday Break, Successful Appeal and Japanese champion miler Hat Trick. 🖎

# Walnut Hall Ltd

Once the motels, restaurants, and filling stations have been left behind, Newtown Pike is almost the road it was a hundred years ago—a place where prize beef cattle and champion horses are raised. One of the most elegant of these farms is historic Walnut Hall Farm, which at one time totaled 3,800 acres of prime Bluegrass farm land. This farm, one of the oldest continuously operating trotting horse farms in the world, has a horse cemetery that reads like a trotters' and pacers' Hall of Fame. Among others buried there are Guy Axworthy, Scotland, and Volomite, the three foundation sires of a Standardbred nursery of such grandeur that historians have declared it "difficult if not impossible to find a harness horse of much note anywhere in the world whose pedigree does not include bloodlines from the farm."

Walnut Hall evolved out of a 3,000-acre land grant made in 1777 by Virginia Governor Patrick Henry to his brother-in-law, Colonel

*Walnut Hall*
3719 Newtown Pike
Lexington, KY 40511
(859) 254-2776

William Christian, as a reward for his services during the French and Indian War. In 1786 Col. Christian was murdered by marauding Indians, and a thousand acres of this land passed to his daughter, Elizabeth, who sold it in 1805 to Walter Warfield. In 1816 Warfield sold it for $10 an acre to Matthew Flournoy, who named it after his French chateau, Fleurnoix. He also built the first house on the farm, which was destroyed by fire in 1842. At his death, his son, Victor, inherited the farm and in the early 1850's he rebuilt the antebellum mansion.

After Victor's death, the farm was sold twice more. In 1891 Lamon Harkness, a native of Connecticut, came to Kentucky seeking trotting horses. He fell in love with the beauty of Walnut Hall and purchased it in 1892. 1992 marked 100 years of continuous ownership by the Harkness family.

Under Harkness's direction, the farm grew to 5,000 acres, and a world-class broodmare operation developed. Harkness built barns and tenant houses and expanded the main house. He also instituted the then unknown practice of selling the farm's crop of yearlings each year at public auction. Harkness valued quality and enjoyed beauty and sought those qualities in everything he owned, whether it was the livestock raised on the farm—cattle, sheep and horses—or the furnishings in his house.

When Harkness died in 1915, the farm passed to his daughter, Lela, wife of Dr. Ogden Edwards. Two years later they made one of the farm's most important purchases when they bought a little-known stallion named Guy Axworthy, whose son and daughter were to be the winners of the first two Hambletonians.

*Walnut Hall Entrance*

*Architectural Detail – Main House*

Dr. Edwards became a world authority in the field of genetics and the breeding of horses. His expertise in Standardbred breeding at Walnut Hall revolutionized the entire industry. When he died in 1941, his wife, Lela Harkness Edwards, continued the operation of the farm with the help of their son, Harkness. Unfortunately, Harkness Edwards died in 1946, and his mother soon thereafter. The farm was ultimately jointly owned by Harkness's widow, Polly, and Dr. and Mrs. Edwards's daughter, Katherine Harkness Edwards Nichols. Polly later married Sherman Jenny, and the decision was made to divide the farm's 3,000 acres. Katherine took 2,000 acres and the Jennys took the 1,000 acres where most of the barns were located. The Jennys renamed their portion Walnut Hall Stud and later sold all but a few acres to the state of Kentucky to be used as a horse park.

Col. Nichols and his wife, Katherine, continued the tradition of breeding outstanding Standardbred horses. They were responsible for breeding Abercrombie, who as a three-year-old, was named Horse of the Year in 1978, and whose lifetime earnings totaled $984,391. Abercrombie was sired by Silent Majority, whose offspring have earned in excess of $26.5 million. (Silent Majority stood at Walnut Hall until his death in August 1992.) Mrs. Nichols, an outstanding horse woman, took an active interest in the operation of the farm. She showed horses and drove Standardbreds, setting a world's record in 1937 that was to stand for more than 20 years when she directed her horse to a 1:59 1/4 win. In 1985, Col. Nichols died, and in 1986 his widow followed. The farm was divided among the Nichols' four daughters. Three of the daughters still operate Standardbred breeding farms on Walnut Hall land. Katherine Sautter and her husband, Dr. James Sautter operate Walnut Hall Stock Farm. Martha Brown operates her part of the farm, which she named Dunroven Stud, with her husband Steve, and Margaret Leavitt and her husband, Allen, own Walnut Hall Limited.

Wildflowers and daffodils surround the main house now located on Walnut Hall Limited. What was once a boardinghouse for the bachelors working on the farm is now used as an office. There are remnants of an ice house that was once stocked with ice chipped out of frozen farm ponds. A tobacco barn, blacksmith shop, machine shop, and horse barns are all painted in Walnut Hall's distinctive butterscotch yellow with maroon roofs. (The main house was also once painted, but was sandblasted so that the original brick is now exposed.) Old carriages, many still usable, are stored in the coach barn, an ornate building with an abundance of gingerbread trim.

Today, Walnut Hall continuously upgrades its broodmare pool, while managing ten stallions, five of which, Cambest (the fastest Standardbred of all time), Garland Lobell, Like A Prayer, Valley Victory, and Victory Dream remain in Lexington. Although the farm's name may have changed, the Walnut Hall tradition of raising quality Standardbred horses continues.

*Mothers of Tomorrow's Triple Crown Winners*

# Horse Tales

# The Bull & the Thoroughbreds

During the early 1800's, in Nicholasville, Kentucky, a gambling gentleman named Major Benjamin Netherland, built a racetrack on his farm where horse races soon were periodically run. After one of these events, Netherland announced an upcoming race that would be run for a $50 purse, which would be open to all animals "with four legs and hair on." Unfortunately for the Major, Michael Arnspiger who worked on the farm, heard the announcement and decided to enter the race with his mount, a saddle-broke bull that hated being spurred.

On the day of the race, upon seeing Arnspiger and the bull, the other contenders cried "foul," but Arnspiger reminded the officials of the Major's announcement and thus was allowed to compete. Arnspiger had chosen for his saddle a large piece of dried ox hide and carried with him a tin horn. When the starting signal was given, he blew on his horn, dug in his spurs, and the bull, bellowing with rage, took off - ox hide saddle flapping in the wind. Not accustomed to such

sights or sounds, the Thoroughbreds ran in every possible direction, except for the finish line. The bull, meanwhile, unimpeded by competition, proceeded calmly to the finish line, where Arnspiger collected the $50 purse.

The losers complained bitterly: if Arnspiger had not had the horn, nor the ox hide saddle, their blooded horses would surely have won, and a repeat match was demanded. Since Arnspiger was a gentleman, he offered to run the race again and agreed to leave the saddle and horn behind.

Again the signal was given and again Arnspiger dug in his spurs. The bull bellowed, the horses scattered, and Arnspiger and the bull trotted to the finish line, where he collected his second $50 purse.

The winnings were put to good use: It is reported that Arnspiger took his money and bought enough equipment to set up a blacksmith shop in Wilmore, Kentucky, which he operated until the 1860's when he died at the age of 85 years.[1]

# John Henry

Photo by Steve Faust   Courtesy Kentucky Horse Park

John Henry: A colt foaled by a little known sire, out of an undistinguished mare. A colt that was first sold for the ridiculously low price of $1,100, to owners who quickly unloaded him for $2,200. A short and dumpy colt whose behavior was so unruly that he had to be gelded before his training could begin. But John Henry was also the horse whose lifetime earnings would exceed $6.5 million, that was twice named Horse of the Year, and that was named by People magazine as one of the "25 most intriguing people of the year."[2]

Born in March 1975 in the Bluegrass region of Kentucky, John Henry was auctioned as a yearling to a Louisville couple who gave him the optimistic name of John Henry, named in honor of the legendary "steel drivin'" man. However, after a less-than-enthusiastic appraisal by their veterinarian, the new owners sold him to Lexington horseman Hal Snowden, Jr., who quickly learned that if John Henry were out in the field, it was safe to approach; however, if he was approached while locked in his stall, it might not be safe to be in the barn at all.  In a mostly unsuccessful attempt to control his behavior, Snowden had him gelded and began to prepare him for his racing career. It wasn't long, however, before he gave up and sold the horse to a Louisiana group. John Henry, a 25-to-1 long shot at the track, could now be had by anyone with the claiming price of $25,000.

No one was interested, and Snowden agreed to take him back.

Thankfully, John Henry's luck was soon to change. Some 750 miles away, Sam Rubin, a New York businessman, was becoming bored. He'd long had an interest in the horse racing business and had put away a stake over the years to satisfy that urge. In early 1978. he heard of John Henry. After talking with Snowden and being assured of the horse's soundness, he mailed his check and the horse was shipped to New York. Rubin was an inexperienced owner, and it is joked that he knew so little of the business that he thought the term "gelded" referred to the color of his new horse. His relationship with John Henry, however, was pure magic.

John Henry won his first race for Rubin at 12-to-1 odds. Throughout the summer and fall, he won 6 out of 13 races, earning more than $120,000. At the ancient age of four—a time when most horses are contemplating retirement—John was given a new trainer, Ron McAnally, and under his guidance, he won his next six races. It soon became evident that he could win on both grass and dirt, carrying all types of weight over many different distances, and that he appeared to enjoy coming from behind to fight off overwhelming odds.

In 1981, John Henry began to race in earnest. He started the year by winning both the San Louis Obispo Handicap and the $400,000 Santa Anita Handicap. He ended it with a record of eight wins out of ten starts. To cap off the year, he was awarded the prestigious Eclipse Award as Horse of the Year, by unanimous vote, a feat which no other horse had achieved in the 11 years of the Award's history. It was also during 1981 that he established a tremendous rapport with his fans. He became the "people's horse" and a "blue collar hero," a horse who gave his all each and every time he was raced.

For the next few years, John Henry continued to race and win. Each time retirement seemed imminent, he would fight back, sweeping the field in race after race. In

*John Henry Doing What He Did Best*

1984 he won the Eclipse Award again and the Arlington Million. Finally, at the age of ten, he was retired—with a career record of 39 victories, 15 seconds and 9 thirds in 83 starts.

John Henry was stabled for 23 years at the Kentucky Horse Park, where he was visited by huge numbers of fans, who would come from all over the country to visit. At Christmas, crates of fruit and carrots arrived, and on his birthday flowers and cakes were sent. A Texas fan vowed to send him a case of carrots every month for the rest of his life, and another local fan delivered a case twice a month. Although some of his admirers never got the chance to see him race, his personality and charisma drew people to him..

In the summer of 2007, John Henry developed serious kidney problems. By October he had stopped responding to treatment, and the decision was made to put him down. On October 8, at the age of 32-1/2, he was humanely euthanized. A few days later, a memorial service was held which was attended by an estimated crowd of 500 people, many of whom were obviously overcome with emotion. Guests, including his former jockey, Chris McCarron, and Sam Rubin's stepson, Tom Levinson, shared their memories of the great champion. He is buried at the park, outside the Hall of Champions.

# Man o' War

*Man o' War Statue now at the Kentucky Horse Park*

On March 29, 1917, at Nursery Stud Farm near Lexington, Kentucky, a beautiful chestnut foal was born. Almost immediately nicknamed "Red" or "Big Red," the foal had been bred by horseman August Belmont II, son of the founder of New York's Belmont Park. Although Belmont originally intended to keep the colt, he ultimately decided to sell this son of Fair Play and Mahubah, along with his other yearling crop at the 1918 Saratoga Yearling Sales. No doubt he regretted this decision for the rest of his life, for this colt was Man o War, the greatest racehorse of the century and the yardstick against which all other horses would be measured for decades.

Man o' War sold for $5,000 and proved to be the bargain of the century for Samuel D. Riddle, owner of Faraway Farm. Three years later, a multimillionaire offered $500,000, then $1,000,000, and finally a blank check for the horse, all of which Riddle refused.

Man o' War ran his first race at Belmont Park on June 19, 1919, winning by six lengths and earning $500. He was beaten only once—on August 13, 1919, in his seventh start—by a horse appropriately named Upset. (He later beat Upset on five separate occasions.) As a three-year-old, he started in 11 stakes races and won them all, setting records in five, equaling one, and establishing a record in another. In three of these races, he carried more than 130 pounds, and in one he carried 138. His lifetime earnings were $249,265, a record at the time. Racehorse followers speculated that the only reason he wasn't a Triple Crown winner was because his owner refused to let him run in the Kentucky Derby. (Riddle believed that there was not sufficient recovery time between the Derby and the Preakness, and that the Derby was too long a distance for a three-year old to run that early in the year.) Big Red was permitted to run in the Preakness and the Belmont and he easily won both. In his last race on October 20, 1920, called by many the race of the century, he ran against Sir Barton, the first Triple Crown winner, and outran him by seven lengths.

Man o' War was a demon on the track, never winning by a nose if he could win by a length, breaking records and the hearts of his competitors with equal ease. He was an athlete that not only wanted to beat his opponents, but wanted to humiliate them as well—once beating an adversary by a quarter of a mile. He ran for the sheer joy of running and won for the joy of winning, and seemed to love the cheers from the crowds who came to see their idol run.

Big Red was retired as a four-year-old to stud duties at Faraway Farm and arrived in Lexington in the fall of 1920. At Faraway, he sired Kentucky Derby winner, Clyde Van Dusen, and Triple Crown winner, War Admiral. His 379 offspring won more than $3.25 million. With Man o' War in residence, Faraway soon became the number one tourist attraction in the state. He and his groom, Will Harbut, charmed the more than 500,000 visitors who came to Faraway each year to pay homage to the fiery horse and listen to Harbut recite his

triumphs. On Man o' War's 21st birthday, celebrities such as "Happy" Chandler, then governor of the state, and others attended the celebration and the festivities were broadcast nationwide.

Will Harbut and Man o' War were friends and companions for over 20 years, but in 1947, both suffered heart attacks. Although Harbut was supposed to remain in his bed, he would slip away each day to visit his friend. Harbut died on October 3, 1947, and in less than a month, at the age of 31, Man o' War followed, some say of a broken heart. Harbut's obituary read in part: "He is survived by his wife, six children, and Man o' War."[3]

Man o' War was embalmed and placed in an oak casket which had been lined with his yellow and black racing colors. He lay in state in the center of his stud barn, where his remains were viewed by thousands of mourners.

His funeral, on November 4, 1947, was attended by over 2,000 people and the services were broadcast nationally. At Churchill Downs a bugler sounded taps and at racetracks across the country tribute was paid. A statue was commissioned and later erected over his grave at Faraway Farm. (In 1974, the statue and Man o' War's remains were moved to the Kentucky Horse Park, where visitors still come each year to pay their respects.)

Nine speakers delivered eulogies at Man o' War's funeral. Sports writer Joe Palmer said, "All horses, and all stallions, like to run, exultant in their strength and power. Most of them run within themselves, as children at play. But Man o' War, loose in his paddock at Faraway, dug in as if the prince of the fallen angels was at his throat-latch... Watching, you felt there had never been, or could ever be again, a horse like this. . .as near to a living flame as horses ever get, and horses get closer to this than anything else."[4] An eloquent tribute, but before he died, Will Harbut said it all when he declared: "He is the Mostes' Hoss in the Whole World." 🐎

# Nancy Hanks

### A Case of Mistaken Identity:

Trotting great Nancy Hanks, named in honor of President Abraham Lincoln's mother, was not only a champion trotter, being the first trotter of either sex to trot a mile in 2:05, but was also extremely successful as a broodmare. Upon her retirement from racing, she was sold to horseman John Madden of Hamburg Place, for whom she produced many Standardbred champions. Madden was so fond of the mare that when she died, she was buried in the center of Hamburg's horseshoe-shaped cemetery, marked with a large stone pedestal and a lovely bronze statue.

According to legend, after President Lincoln's assassination, several mourners came to Lexington to pay homage to his mother. Upon asking directions to Nancy Hanks's grave, many Lexingtonians, being more familiar with racing than with politics, assumed inquirers were looking for the trotter's grave and so gave directions to Hamburg Place. Once there, the visitors humbly climbed the stone wall bordering the cemetery and reverently hung wreaths around the neck of the small bronze statue, wondering perhaps why a statute of a horse was chosen to honor the President's mother.

The graveyard has since been moved a few feet and now abuts Sir Barton Way in Lexington, Kentucky. Upon completion of the cemetery's restoration, scheduled for 2008, it will once again be open to the public.[5]

*Mare and Foal — A Familiar Bluegrass Sight*

# Seattle Slew

*Statue at Three Chimneys Farm*

In 1974 a dark bay foal was born on the White Horse Acres farm in Lexington, Kentucky. The foal was so ungainly, had a head so big and legs so long, that there was little, if any evidence of the champion he was to become. At auction the next year, few were perceptive enough to see the possibilities of the young colt. But in true storybook fashion, the ugly duckling was bought by Mickey and Karen Taylor,

beginners in the horse racing business, and Jim Hill, with whom the Taylors had recently formed a partnership. Jim Hill, a veterinarian, had been trained at the New Bolton Center, University of Pennsylvania. The Taylors were from Yakima, Washington, where Karen had been an airline hostess, and Mickey a logging truck driver until he struck it big in the wood pulp business. Although Mickey was violently allergic to horses, the Taylors had always loved them and were now able to indulge their passion. The Taylors had met Hill at a yearling auction in 1974, and subsequently became partners, forming Wooden Horse Investment. And in 1975, the partners attended a Kentucky yearling sale, where they were to buy—for $17,500--this funny-looking colt.

The colt was so funny-looking, in fact, that when his new trainer, Paula Turner, first saw him, she immediately dubbed him "Baby Huey," a nickname that stuck. Baby Huey proved himself to be a good-tempered colt, clumsy and lovable, though strong and mischievous. After the colt was broke, Paula's husband, Billy, took over the colt's training.

Exercise rider Mike Kennedy was not immediately impressed with this colt whose legs seemed to head in every direction at once. However, in September 1976, Huey was entered in his first race at New York's Belmont Racetrack. He won easily. In October he was entered in another race at Belmont. Again, he won easily. With some hesitation, it was decided to enter the horse in the $125,000 Champagne Stakes, the richest contest for juveniles in the state. Not only did he win, but he ran in record time, winning by almost ten lengths and earning $82,350. In three races, he was named Champion Two-Year-Old Colt, had the racing world's attention, and was no longer known as "the ugly duckling."

Seattle Slew was rested over the winter in preparation for his three-year-old career, which he launched with a record-breaking win at Florida's Hialeah track. He then won the $100,000 Flamingo Stakes, finishing 4-1/2 lengths ahead of the field. He continued to race and win, while the "Slew Crew" (as his owners and trainers were called) planned for May's Kentucky Derby. Seattle Slew won both the Derby and the Preakness. In June, he headed for New York and the 1.5 mile Belmont Stakes, the longest of the three races, where many Triple Crown dreams have been dashed. Seattle Slew was first all the way, becoming not just the tenth Triple Crown winner, but also the first to win the honor undefeated.

Seattle Slew was defeated as a three-year-old, but was named champion as a four-year-old. In November 1978, with life-time earnings of $1,208,726 (69 times his purchase price), he was retired to stud duties at Spendthrift Farm. He was syndicated for $12,000,000, and later moved to Three Chimneys Farm, where he stood for 17 years. In April 2002 he was moved to Hill n' Dale Farm to recuperate from surgery. The next month, on the 25th anniversary of his Kentucky Derby win, Slew died in his sleep at the age of 26 years.

*There are approximately 38.7 miles of stone fence still standing in Fayette County. It is generally believed that these fences were built by Irish stone masons who immigrated to the area during the early 1800's, and that although some of the fences were built with slave labor, their work was directed by these Irish immigrants. Following the Civil War, freed slaves with masonry skills were hired to build these popular fences. The availability of skilled labor, an abundance of limestone, the need for strong fences, and the appreciation of the fences' natural beauty led to the construction of these fences in the Bluegrass area.*

*View from Clovelly Farm barn*

# The Horse's World

# Breeding A Champion

The ultimate goal for most horse breeding operations is to produce a foal that will become both a fast racehorse and a successful sire. Not only must a successful stud farm keep this goal in mind, it must also ensure that everything possible has been done to eliminate any danger to these valuable animals.

There are many risks involved in horse breeding. Sexually-transmitted disease, such as Contagious Equine Metritis (C.E.M), can prevent conception. A stallion could bite or otherwise unwittingly injure a mare as he mounts her. An agitated and unwilling mare, delivering a well-aimed kick, could bring a stallion's breeding life to an abrupt and painful end. Human life is at risk as well, for if one of these horses were to kick, bite, or suddenly fall, a person could be

seriously injured or killed.

At Three Chimneys Farm, one of the Bluegrass region's outstanding breeding establishments, safety is of utmost importance. The breeding shed floor is covered with a thick carpet of shredded wood fibers which provides cushioning and traction. To negate any height differences between the mare and the stallion (which would make breeding even more difficult and dangerous), there is a gradual incline in the floor, allowing the mare to be placed at an appropriate level. The chips in this area are covered with a mat, providing even more security for the horses.

Each breeding must be videotaped and witnessed as proof that the scheduled breeding did take place and that no damage was done by, or to, either horse. Immediately after the breeding, a small

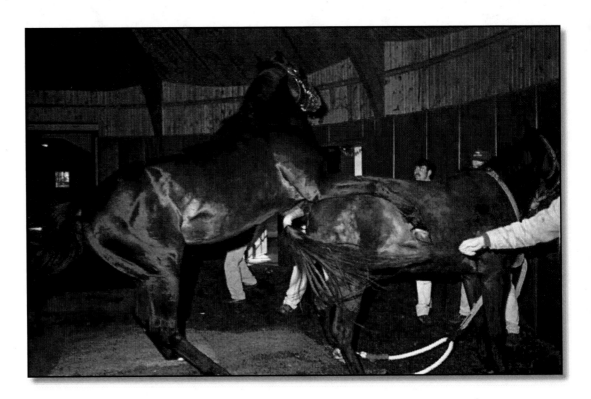

Seattle Slew

amount of semen is collected and examined by microscope to confirm the presence of live sperm.

On this day, in the early 1990's, evidence of spring's arrival is everywhere. Birds are building nests, trees and flowers are budding, and newborn foals are playing in the fields. Inside the breeding shed, the rites of spring are also being observed as Three Chimneys prepares to breed its extremely valuable superstar, Seattle Slew. Four men will assist, and although they are well-trained, the atmosphere is still tense.

Prior to the mare's arrival at the shed, she is introduced to a teaser that determines her readiness for breeding. If she is found to be in season, about 14" of her tail is bound to help hold it out of the stallion's way, and her vaginal area is washed with an antiseptic solution to inhibit the transmission of disease. The mare is then led into the shed through the back entrance and positioned at the appropriate level on the mound, with her nose almost touching the rear wall. The men quickly slip padded boots onto her rear feet in the event she should manage to kick and add a hobble to limit her ability to do so. Not until she is properly prepared is Seattle Slew brought into the room.

Seattle Slew is an experienced stallion and knows exactly what's expected of him and rears and snorts to show his readiness. He is led to the mare and guided into place. In a few seconds, the breeding is complete and the mare is docilely led away. As she left, it was hard not to hope that maybe next year another champion—maybe even another Triple Crown winner—will be born to play in the fields at Three Chimneys.

---

*Many times small farm animals are used as stall companions for racehorses as they tend to have a calming effect on these high-strung animals. Goats, in particular, are ideal for this purpose. However, a horse can become so attached to his stablemate that he may become distraught and agitated if the goat is removed. Therefore, if a person wished to upset the horse and place his competitor at a disadvantage, he might arrange for the goat to be stolen—hence, the expression "got his goat."*

◇◇◇◇◇◇◇◇◇◇◇◇◇◇◇◇◇◇◇◇◇◇◇◇◇◇◇◇◇◇◇◇◇◇◇◇◇◇◇◇◇◇◇◇◇◇◇◇◇◇◇◇◇◇◇◇◇◇◇◇

*If a colt is born on January 1, 1991, he becomes one year old on January 1, 1992. Likewise, a colt born on December 31, 1991, will also become one year old on January 1, 1992. Therefore, most horse farms try to schedule breedings so that the foals are born as close as possible to the beginning of the new year.*

# Horse Haven Farm

## Horse Haven Farm

4895 Buggy Lane
Lexington, Kentucky
(859) 293-6785
www.horsehavenfarm.com

Horse Haven Farm is a high-tech equine center that prides itself on providing excellent convalescent, rehabilitative, and reconditioning services. If a horse needs to be quarantined, Horse Haven has the facilities to keep each horse the mandated 30' apart. If it needs stall rest or is recovering from surgery, there are six 12' x 14' stalls and two 14' x 14' stalls that are continuously monitored. If an owner has concerns about a mare who's about to foal, she can be brought to the center for care.

The idea for the center grew out of owner Stephen Corbin's experiences when his own horse needed long-term care. Having grown up with horses, he knows the importance of good health care and envisioned a facility where he would feel comfortable leaving his own horse.

The convalescent facility is state of the art. Each stall is filled with shredded cardboard which is soft and biodegradable. There are automatic watering stations with consumption indicators to help prevent dehydration. Each stall contains an automatic fly sprayer, ceiling fan, heated waterer, and feed dish. Cameras are mounted in each stall so that both caretakers and owners can monitor the horses through the farm's web site. There is a central vacuum system, surround sound, and an intercom system that is connected to the Corbins' home.

Humidity and temperature are constantly monitored, and a geo-thermal system maintains a winter temperature of 75 degrees, a summer temperature of 70 degrees, and a relative humidity of 40-55 percent. The kitchen where special diets are mixed is immaculate - as is the rest of the facility. Two high tech wash bays with a selection of soaps (regular, extra clean, whitening, and conditioner) and a spray nozzle to lift the horse's hair so soap can reach the skin and still be easily rinsed, are conveniently located near the stalls.

The staff, which includes both Veterinarian Molly Metz and Veterinary Technician Mike Mueller, works together closely to ensure continuity of care. The Internet is also used when necessary

*Inside Barn*

to transmit pictures of anything that might look suspicious. In addition to using the latest technology, the center offers natural, alternative methods of treatment. To speed the healing process, the center offers such services as equine massage, which helps reduce stress and increase flexibility, provided by Keith Spears; Reiki, a complementary technique which helps increase healing energy, with Christine Austin; and acupuncture, which can help relieve pain and joint inflammation, with Dr. Claire Seagren.

Located right outside the stable area is an exercise ring with a 50' Odyssey walker and exerciser that can accommodate up to four horses, as well as a 50' round pen where training, using the John Lyons conditioned response method (also known as the soft touch technique) begins. Most horses will receive from 30 to 60 days of greenbreak training so that they can understand basic commands and be comfortable with a rider.

In addition to convalescent services, Horse Haven also offers stallion services (Master Ile De Slew, a grandson of Mr. Prospector and out of a Seattle Slew mare). As a separate venture, they sell not only St. Bernards, but Bennett's Wallabies (miniature kangaroos) as well. They currently have two on hand, which are friendly and playful.

*One of Horse Haven's Wallabies*

Although many of the horses in the Bluegrass region are not expensive Thoroughbreds, their owners care about them and want them to receive the best treatment available. Horse Haven Farm is a good example of the type of care that is available to these beloved animals.

# Keeneland Association

There are few better places in all the Bluegrass—perhaps in all Kentucky - to spend a day than at the Keeneland race course. Even for those who don't particularly care for the sport of kings, there's plenty to see and do. Visitors are encouraged to arrive in time to watch the horses' early morning workouts, and for nature lovers, the grounds are beautiful throughout the year. Even the parking lot has been declared the most beautiful lot in North America.

The facilities at Keeneland are superb. Classified as a National Historic Landmark in 1986, this 997-acre showplace has 57 barns housing up to 1,951 horses, walking rings, and a state of the art racetrack with a synthetic racing surface known as Polytrack, which is designed to provide a safer ride for both horse and jockey. Horses are exercised and trained year-round between the hours of 6 a.m. until 10 a.m., and the public is invited to watch from choice grandstand seating. A good morning would include a stroll around the grounds, breakfast at the Track Kitchen, and then settling in at the grandstand for a semi-private performance. During the April and October race meets you can lunch on Keeneland's legendary burgoo, corned beef sandwiches and bread pudding at concession stands. The gift shop

### Keeneland Association
4201 Versailles Road
Lexington, Kentucky
(800) 456-3412 or (859) 254-3412
www.keeneland.com

is a great spot throughout the year to pick up a unique souvenir to commemorate the excursion to Keeneland.

Keeneland can also boast of having one of the world's largest Thoroughbred libraries. Established in 1939 and greatly expanded over the years, this extensive collection of equine literature is open to the public. A new state-of-the-art library was opened in 2002 to house the collection of the Daily Racing Form and Morning Telegraph dating back to the mid-1800's - many of which are sole surviving copies.

Keeneland, a combination racetrack, sales company and training facility, traces its beginnings to the early 1900's, when John Oliver Keene, owner of Keeneland farm, decided to build at Keeneland a training facility to accommodate both horses and horsemen. The foundation of the great stone building was laid in 1916 with construction proceeding intermittently for the next 15 years with the greatest portion accomplished in the late 1920's. The centerpiece of his vision was a great "barn" that was to be the grandest in all Kentucky. Designed for men and horses alike, the barn was to have three stories, 48 stalls, an indoor training track, and living quarters for Keene and his guests.

With the Great Depression, Keene's ability to fund the project was diminished and construction came to a standstill with the exception of the track itself which

*Call to Post*

was finished in 1931. By then, Keene had invested over $400,000 dollars - a fortune at the time - and had begun using the facilities as a training center. It was his stated hope that ultimately the track would be taken over by an organization of dedicated sportsmen as a public course and operated for sport only and without profit.

Coincidentally, in 1933 the regional racetrack, the Kentucky Association, closed and several noted Kentucky horsemen formed a nonprofit corporation for the purpose of building the finest racetrack in the country. Their goals, as formally stated, were to establish a model race track dedicated solely to the perpetuation and improvement of the sport. The association members surveyed numerous available properties for the new race track, narrowed their selection quickly and after negotiations were complete, purchased 145-acres of Keene's property including all improvements, the racetrack, "a great stone building" and stone fence.

After the purchase in June 1935, the transformation began. The great stone building became what is now the clubhouse, and the horse stalls and guest rooms became

offices and dining rooms. At the track's entrance, an iron post from the original Kentucky Association track bearing the signature laurel wreath and initials KA was placed to identify the new "Keeneland Association" racetrack. During renovations, the builders scavenged steel, seats and barns from the old track and hauled away other usable building material with a goal of opening the new racing plant with little or no debt remaining after construction.

By October of 1936, renovations were complete, and Keeneland had its first race meeting. Since that time, the track has opened each year, with the exception of war years, to avid racing enthusiasts from all over the world who come to watch Thoroughbred racing at its finest. During World War II, the spring meeting was held at Churchill Downs and the fall meeting was canceled. Today, a stakes race is run each day of the spring meet, and the purse for one of the most important Kentucky Derby prep races, the Toyota Blue Grass Stakes, has grown to $750,000.

*Jockeys Await Mounts*

Although now a for-profit company, Keeneland pays no dividends as all earnings are reinvested and used for such necessities as capital improvements, higher purses, and industry innovations. In addition, true to its original not-for-profit mission, Keeneland donates much of its profits to charitable causes. Since the 1930's, Keeneland has given back more than $16 million to the central Kentucky community, in recent years averaging over a million dollars annually to worthy organizations.

Thanks to the foresight of the track's founding fathers and the dedication of the supporters who have guided the track since its early inception, Keeneland does live up to its classic motto, ***"Racing as it was meant to be."***

*Horse and Jockey*

***Meets:***
Three Weeks in Both April and October.
Racing Daily Wednesday through Sunday.

***Post Time:***
1:15 p.m. • Gates open at 11:00 a.m.

***Admission:***
Grandstand $3.00
Reserved Seats $3-W/Th/F; $5-S/S; $12 Toyota

***Bluegrass Stakes Day***
Clubhouse admission only by annual membership
or as guest of a member.

***Parking:*** Free

# Kentucky Horse Park

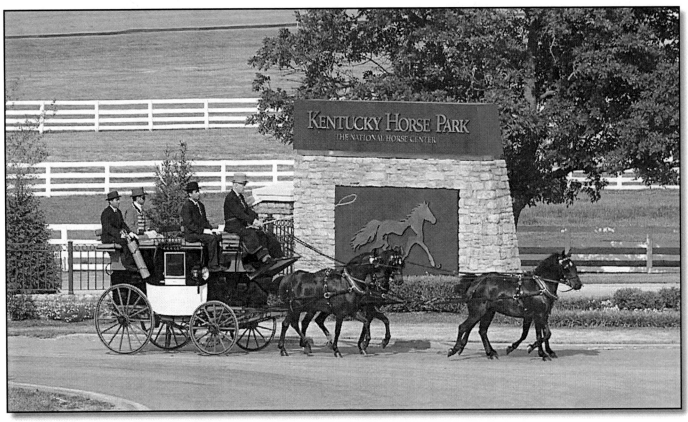

*Photo by Marc Manning  Courtesy Kentucky Horse Park*

## Kentucky Horse Park
4089 Iron Works Parkway
Lexington, Kentucky 40511
(859) 233-4303
www.kyhorsepark.com

Set on more than 1,200 rolling acres, and surrounded by more than 30 miles of white plank fences, the Kentucky Horse Park is an idyllic icon of the famous Bluegrass region of Kentucky and is a family-friendly attraction where tourists can enjoy a "hands-on" visit with the park's almost 50 different breeds of horse.

A majestic bronze statue of legendary Thoroughbred Man o' War welcomes visitors at the entrance to the park. Directly behind is the Visitor Information Center, where detailed information regarding park activities can be obtained. The admission fee covers the basic attractions of the park: the International Museum of the Horse and the American Saddlebred Museum; a visit to the Draft Barn, where such breeds as Belgians, Clydesdales, and Percherons are stabled; a self-guided walking tour where visitors can see a blacksmith at work; and live presentations such as the Parade of Breeds, where various breeds are ridden by costumed handlers, and the Hall of Champions Show, where famous horses such as Cigar meet the public. Throughout the park, visitors have a chance to get close to horses, pet them, and talk with their handlers.

Paid attractions include horseback and pony rides, and a tour of some of the area horse farms. (Some outdoor activities are available

mid-March through October 31 only. Detailed information is available at www. kyhorsepark.com.)

Throughout the year there are also special events such as the Rolex Kentucky Three-Day Event, polo, steeplechase races, rodeos and concerts.  The park is also home of the Alltech FEI World Equestrian Games 2010, which will run from September 25 to October 10, 2010.  This is the first time that the event is to be held outside Europe and it will be the largest equine sporting event ever held in the United States.

Billed as "THE place to get close to horses," a visit to the park is an experience that can be enjoyed by both the novice and experienced equestrian. Conveniently located 5 miles north of Lexington, lodging is available at a number of hotels located near the park.  In addition, there is a resort-style campground with full hook-up and swimming pool, and a restaurant and gift shop located in the main park.

*Rolex Three Day Event Competitor*

# North American Racing Academy

*Classroom Work*

## North American Racing Academy

3380 Paris Pike
Lexington, KY 40511
(859) 294-6485

There was one in Japan, one in Ireland, and one in Australia, but there wasn't one in the United States – one of the few countries where Thoroughbreds are raced that did not have one. Although several area horsemen had considered the idea, it wasn't until Hall of Fame jockey Chris McCarron got involved that the first formal school for jockeys was born in the United States – appropriately located in the Bluegrass region of Kentucky.

Among other successes, McCarron has won two Kentucky Derbys and was a regular rider of superhorse John Henry. After retiring from racing, he stayed connected with the sport as vice president and general manager of the Santa Anita racetrack in California. For 15 years, though, he had been concerned about the lack of formal training available to jockeys in the United States. Having been a part of the sport for so many years, he knew that most jockeys move up the ladder by learning how to break and exercise horses at the farms, or, for the lucky ones, by finding qualified mentors who have the time, skill, and expertise to teach them. Even with that help, it can still take about 10 to 15 years for a jockey to reach his peak as a rider.

In February 2005, having had several conversations with officials at Keeneland and the Kentucky Horse Park, McCarron visited the Bluegrass to scout potential locations for the school. A few months later it was announced that initial training and academic subjects would be held at the Horse Park, and that more advanced riding skills would be taught at The Thoroughbred Center. With that, the North American Racing Academy was launched.

The first students – 11 (7 men, 4 women) – started in September 2006. Each was assigned a horse for which they would be responsible. Of the 11, only a few had ever been on a horse before, but all advanced from learning how to muck a stall to galloping racehorses. They studied equine science and horse physiology, and academic subjects such as math, science, nutrition, and personal finance. The Academy is affiliated with the Bluegrass Community & Technical College and, therefore, can offer a two-year associates degree, which requires about 74 hours of college work. Midway

*McCarron and Friend*

through their last year, students are sent on internships for hands-on experience. Taking advantage of his connections with the horse industry, McCarron arranges these internships at tracks across the country so that students can benefit from the tutelage of experienced horse trainers and owners.

Students come from all over the country and Canada. In addition to basic horse maintenance, they've learned how to tack a horse and how to sit a saddle. They've also learned that if they ride long enough, they will, no doubt, fall off. More importantly, they've seen first hand that there's more to riding a horse than just climbing on, and that steering a 1,000 pound animal takes way more strength than steering a car. The Academy stresses the importance of good nutrition and uses Equicizers to build strength and fitness. These machines, which simulate an actual horse ride, are the same machines that jockeys use to get back in shape after a long lay off from the track. It's hard work and most of the students are tired and sweaty by the end of a workout.

The Academy's stated mission is ". . . to develop and operate a world-class racing

*Mucking a Stall*

school that will provide students with the education, training and experience needed to become skilled in the art of race riding, proficient in the care and management of racehorses, and knowledgeable about the workings of the racing industry as a whole. Under McCarron's guidance, and with the help of his enthusiastic, knowledgeable staff, the Academy has come a long way towards meeting those goals.

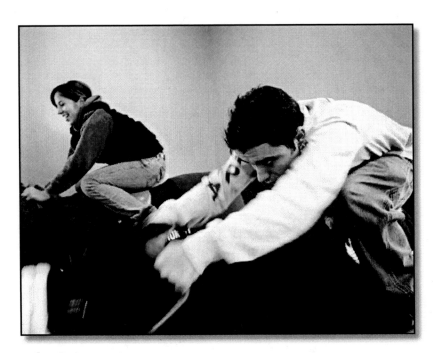

*Building Muscle the Hard Way*

*There are approximately 1,000 horse farms in Kentucky, 300 of which are located in Fayette County. Horse farms are also located in 108 of the state's 120 counties.*

# The Red Mile

Picture ten powerful horses pulling sulkies with drivers in brilliant racing colors. Add the sound of thousands of pounds of horseflesh hitting a dirt track, mix with the screams of the crowd, stir in the thrill of the race, and you've got a recipe for an unforgettable event.

The first organized harness races in this area were spontaneous competitions when young gentlemen raced their light-harness horses on the streets of downtown Lexington. The first official harness race in Lexington, however, was held during the Fayette County Fair of 1850. Interest was so great that by the late 1850's, a trotting association had been formed and a racetrack built. When the Civil War erupted, harness racing was temporarily suspended as the track was confiscated for camp sites by Union and Confederate soldiers in turn. In addition, blooded horses were often confiscated for war duty, and in order to protect their prized stock, cautious breeders stayed away from any organized races.

After the war ended, harness racing again became popular, and on October 16, 1872, a four-day meet was held at the original track. The event was a huge success, and in 1875 the land on which the original track was situated was traded for the property where The Red Mile Harness Track is now located. On September 28, 1875, the Great Fall Trots officially opened The Red Mile, which remains the second oldest harness track in the world..

To increase the winners' purses and to improve the caliber of horses raced, the Trotting Association instituted stakes races. The most prestigious and the oldest stakes race in the harness world is the Kentucky Futurity, begun in 1893. In

## The Red Mile
1200 Red Mile Road
Lexington, KY
(859) 255-0752
www.theredmile.com

1955 the Futurity was coupled with the Hambletonian and the Yonkers Trot to form trotting's "Triple Crown" of racing. Today, harness racing in Lexington begins with the May stakes races and culminates with the "Grand Circuit," in which the best of the best race. The Grand Circuit runs from the last week in September through the first week in October, and on the last day the Futurity is raced. In 2004, the Red Mile hosted its inaugural Quarter Horse meet, the first time that Quarter-horses have raced in the Bluegrass in more than a decade.

Harness racing is a family-oriented sport, one that is not limited to the affluent. Although a Standardbred can cost thousands of dollars, a good one can sometimes be bought at bargain prices, and the cost of training and maintaining the horse is comparatively reasonable.

The Red Mile is more than just a racetrack. A museum, the "Standardbred Stable of Memories," is housed in historic Floral Hall, built in 1879 by local architect John McMurtry. The Historic Round Barn, listed on the National Register of Historic Places, and The Clubhouse can be rented for dinners, weddings, and other events.

Paddock Park, where the horses are paraded before races, can be used for picnics. Throughout the year, the facilities are used for such special events as Bluegrass music festivals, chili cook-offs, and concerts by the local philharmonic orchestra. The Red Mile simulcasts 365 days a year. Visitors are welcome at morning workouts and special tours can be arranged. 🕊

The year 1992 was a banner year for the sport of horse racing in communist countries. On April 26, 1992, the first horse race to be run in China since its takeover by communist forces was held, with capitalism a clear winner, as thousands of dollars were bet by over 5,000 Chinese racing enthusiasts. And for the first time, in May 1992, the running of the Kentucky Derby was shown live, complete with commercials, in Russia.

◇◇◇◇◇◇◇◇◇◇◇◇◇◇◇◇◇◇◇◇◇◇◇◇◇◇◇◇◇◇◇◇◇◇◇◇◇◇◇◇◇◇◇◇◇◇◇◇◇◇◇◇◇◇◇◇◇◇

It was once believed that eagles brought good luck at the racetrack; therefore, several horse farms have mounted masonry eagles at their entrance gates.

◇◇◇◇◇◇◇◇◇◇◇◇◇◇◇◇◇◇◇◇◇◇◇◇◇◇◇◇◇◇◇◇◇◇◇◇◇◇◇◇◇◇◇◇◇◇◇◇◇◇◇◇◇◇◇◇◇◇

Although no one is sure just why, a horseshoe nailed over a door is supposed to ward off back luck. If a person should have the good fortune to find a horseshoe, he should immediately return to his house, without speaking to anyone, and fasten the shoe over the door with three nails, each of which is hit three times with the hammer. The shoe must be fastened prongs up or else the luck will fall out.

# The Thoroughbred Center

In September 1969, local veterinarian Arnold Pessin and California horseman Rex Ellsworth unveiled their plans for a $3 million Thoroughbred horse complex housing a training center, a boarding facility with 900 stalls, and an auction arena,. There were to be two training tracks—a 7/8 mile track and a 5/8-mile track, two barns, and a state-of-the-art sales pavilion.

The Thoroughbred Center has become all that was planned and more. Changing hands several times over the years, barns and other buildings have been added, additional acreage purchased, and the main facility has undergone a $1,000,000 restoration. Major capitol improvements include resurfacing of both tracks, installation of extensive drainage systems, and construction of a

## The Thoroughbred Center

3380 Paris Pike
Lexington, Kentucky
(859) 293-1853
www.thethoroughbredcenter.com

*Statue in Front of Thoroughbred Center*

security guard house, a spectator viewing stand, a tour office, and maintenance buildings. Other improvements such as wash pads with drains, grass gallop areas, signage, exterior lighting, landscaping, van parking and loading area were also made. In April 2000, the Center was purchased by the Keeneland Association. Originally known as the Kentucky Horse Center, during the transition the name was changed to The Thoroughbred Center. Today, the Center can house up to 1,188 horses, with more than 30 barns. The 7/8-mile training track has a 6-stall electric starting gate, and the 5/8-mile track has a 4-stall gate.

According to Jim Pendergest, TTC's General Manager, assuming good physical condition, a yearling can usually be trained for racing within six to eight months (although he cannot be raced until he becomes a two-year-old) and a two-year-old can be trained in four to five months. Stabling fees are moderate and are considered a bargain by area horsemen as costs for stabling at racetracks across the country have increased. Stabling at TTC also allows trainers the flexibility of racing on a Kentucky circuit while maintaining a more traditional family lifestyle by staying in one location on a year-round basis.

The administrative facilities at TTC can be rented. In addition to horse sales, the 900-seat sales pavilion is used for corporate meetings, fund raisers, concerts and other public events. The lounge area and two conference rooms are well-suited for private parties, receptions, and small meetings.

Escorted tours are available from Monday through Saturday, April 1 through October 31, and Monday through Friday from November 2 through March 31. Tours last approximately an hour and a half and are scheduled to begin at 9:00 a.m. Individual cost is $10.00 per adult and $5.00 per child age 12 and under. (Group rates are available.) Since space is limited, prepaid reservations are recommended.

# Thoroughbred Park

*Children at Play*

Completed in April 1992, Thoroughbred Park is one of the country's most unique cultural landmarks—it is a park completely designed and dedicated to pay tribute to the horse. Under construction for over a year, the $8-million-dollar park was constructed with donations made by civic-minded corporations and private citizens. In addition to the horse statutes, its 2.75 acres feature 247 trees, a multi-jetted fountain, a reflecting pool, and a large planter filled with Kentucky Derby roses and other flowers representative of the Triple Crown races.

In front of a dry-laid stone wall are bronze equine statutes sculpted by local artist Gwen Reardon, each of which weighs hundreds of pounds. There are seven racing Thoroughbreds with riders—jockeys Willie Shoemaker, Pat Day, Chris McCarron, Randy Romero, Don Brumfield, Jerry Bailey and Craig Perret, who wear bronze racing silks cast by Reardon from actual silks donated by well-known racing stables. Cast life-size, these statues are so realistic that while on display at a Santa Fe racetrack, horses out for early morning walks were spooked, thinking they were being led into a horse race-in-progress. There is a half-size statue of the greatest Thoroughbred sire of his day, the stallion Lexington, and as a tribute to the next generation of racing champions, two broodmares, two foals, and one newborn now "graze" on a small berm overlooking the fountain.

The park is open year-round and there is no admission charge. 🦢

## Thoroughbred Park

410 East Main
Lexington, Kentucky

# Lexington - Fayette County

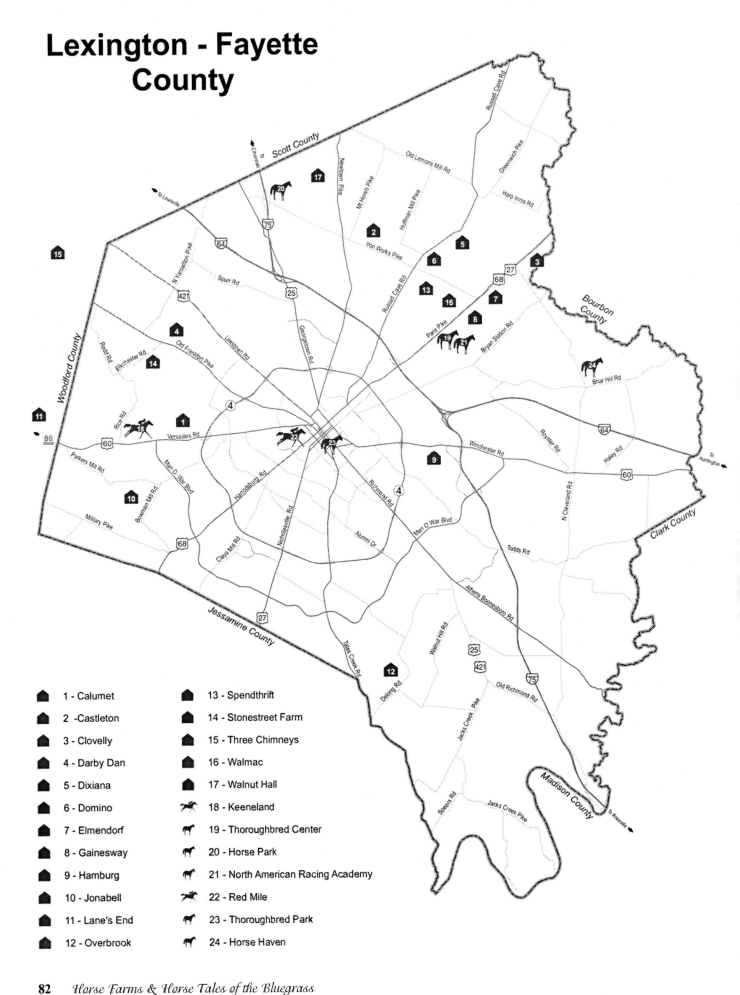

1 - Calumet

2 -Castleton

3 - Clovelly

4 - Darby Dan

5 - Dixiana

6 - Domino

7 - Elmendorf

8 - Gainesway

9 - Hamburg

10 - Jonabell

11 - Lane's End

12 - Overbrook

13 - Spendthrift

14 - Stonestreet Farm

15 - Three Chimneys

16 - Walmac

17 - Walnut Hall

18 - Keeneland

19 - Thoroughbred Center

20 - Horse Park

21 - North American Racing Academy

22 - Red Mile

23 - Thoroughbred Park

24 - Horse Haven

# Horse Terms

# Glossary of Equine Terminology

**ALLOWANCE RACE:** Event in which eligibility to enter and/or weight to be carried by each horse are determined by a horse's previous race record. For example, "open to non-winners of two races," or "weight: 122 pounds, non-winners of a race since January 1 allowed three pounds (carry three pounds less)." Allowance races generally are considered of a higher class than claiming races, but of a lower class than stakes, although some stakes can be run under allowance conditions.

**BARREN MARE:** A mare that was bred, but that did not conceive during previous breeding season.

**BAY:** Brown or tan horse with black mane and tail.

**BLACK:** The entire coat of the horse is black, including the muzzle, flanks, mane, and tail. White leg markings can be present.

**BLACK TYPE:** Bold face type, often used in sales catalogs, to distinguish horses that have won or placed in a stakes race. If a horse's name appears in bold-face type, with all capital letters, he has won at least one stakes. If it appears in bold-face type with capital and lowercase letters, he has placed in at least one stakes.

**BLANKET OF ROSES:** A garland of roses which is draped over the neck of the winner of the Kentucky Derby.

**BLEEDER:** A horse which, during or following exercise, bleeds from its lungs. The condition is generally not considered to be serious as it can be controlled with medication such as Lasix.

**BLOODED HORSE:** A Thoroughbred horse.

**BLUE GRASS STAKES:** A 1-1/8 mile prep race for the Kentucky Derby.

**BOOK:** The group of mares being bred to a stallion in one given year. If he attracts the maximum number of mares allowed by his manager (usually about 40), he has a full book.

**BROODMARE:** A female horse that has been bred and is used to produce foals.

**BROODMARE SIRE:** The father of a horse's dam, also called the maternal grandsire.

**COLT:** An uncastrated male four years old or younger.

**CONSIGNOR:** The person who offers a horse for sale through auction.

**CRIBBER:** Horse that bites parts of its stall, sucking air into its lungs.

**CROP:** The group of foals sired during a stallion's season at stud. Also a short, stiff whip used by jockeys during horse races.

**DAM:** Female parent.

**DARK BAY OR BROWN:** The entire coat of the horse varies from a brown with areas of tan on the shoulders, head and flanks, to a dark brown with tan areas only evident on the flanks and/or muzzle. Mane, tail and lower legs are always black unless white markings are present.

**DEAD HEAT:** A tie for finishing position, officially called when the judges, using a photo-finish camera, cannot separate two horses.

**DERBY:** A 1-1/4 mile stakes race restricted to three-year-old horses, and the first leg in the Thoroughbred Triple Crown.

**ECLIPSE AWARDS:** Since 1971, given to North American divisional champions each year after having been voted upon by the *Daily Racing Form*, Thoroughbred Racing Association, and National Turf Writers Association.

**FILLY:** A female horse four years old or younger.

**FOAL:** A young horse of either sex in its first year of life.

**FULL BROTHER (SISTER):** Horses who have both the same sires and dams.

**FURLONG:** One-eighth of a mile (220 yards). From the English phrase "furrow long," which is the length of a plowed field.

**CANNON BONE:** The bone located between the knee or hock and the fetlock and a common site of fracture in race horses.

**CHESTNUT:** A brown horse, with mane and tail of similar color.

**CHURCHILL DOWNS:** Located in Louisville, Kentucky, and home of the Kentucky Derby for over a century.

**CLAIMING RACE:** An event in which each horse entered is eligible to be purchased at a set price. Claims must be made before the race and only by licensed owners who have a horse registered to race at that meeting, or who have received a claim certificate from the steward. Claiming races are generally of a lower class than allowance races. Also, the lower the claiming price, the lower the class.

**GELDING**: A male horse of any age that has had both testicles removed.

**HORSE:** A generic term for an equine animal. When reference is made to sex, a "horse" is an uncastrated male five years old or older.

**INQUIRY:** A review of the conduct of a race, asked for by the judges. The inquiry light appears on the Tote Board in this situation.

**JOCKEY CLUB, THE:** The national official registrar of the Thoroughbred breed, headquartered in Lexington, Kentucky, who is also the adopter of a national set of racing rules. No North American-bred Thoroughbred can race without receiving registration papers from this organization. Individual states' racing rules are basically the same as those of The Jockey Club.

**JUVENILE:** A two-year-old racehorse, the youngest age one can compete in races.

**KENTUCKY FUTURITY:** The Kentucky Futurity, Hambletonian, and the Yonkers Trot form the trotting world's Triple Crown.

**LIVE FOAL GUARANTEE:** Usually the breeding contract provision which guarantees the owner of the mare a live, standing, nursing foal as a result of the purchased breeding. The guarantee usually gives the mare owner the right to re-breed the next season to the same stallion should his mare not produce a live foal during the current season.

**LUNGING AREA:** An enclosed exercise area.

**MAIDEN:** Either a race horse of either sex that has never won a race or a female horse that has never been bred. Also a classification of race open only to horses that have never won a race. Straight (non-claiming) maiden races are considered of a higher class than maiden claiming races.

**MAIDEN MARE:** A mare that has not been bred. The term is also often used to refer to mares carrying their first foals.

**MARE:** A female horse that is five years old or older.

**OPEN MARE:** A mare (other than a maiden mare) that was not bred during the previous breeding season.

**OUTSIDE MARE:** A mare that is not owned by the farm where she is being boarded or bred.

**PACER:** A Standardbred whose legs move in tandem: left front and rear, and right front and rear. Also called "sidewheelers." Plastic loops called "hobbles" are used to keep the legs synchronized. Pacers are usually several seconds faster than trotters.

**PHOTO FINISH:** A race where horses finish within 1/2 length of each other, requiring the judges to study a photo to determine the order of finish.

**POOL:** The total amount of money bet on all of the horses in a particular race.

**ROAN:** The majority of the horse's coat is a mixture of red and white hairs. The mane, tail and legs may be black, chestnut or roan unless white markings are present.

**SADDLEBRED:** Originating in Kentucky, these horses were bred for high intelligence, a fast walk, easy canter, clear trot, and a learned gait. Thoroughbred crosses are generally found in the bloodlines of these horses; however, the neck must be arched, and the horse must have a much calmer and more docile temperament. Also known as "saddlers" and show horses.

**SCRATCH:** A horse that is withdrawn from a race.

**SIRE:** The male parent of a horse.

**SOPHOMORE:** A three-year-old racehorse.

**SOUND:** The condition of a horse that is free of lameness, injury or illness.

**STAKES:** A race in which an entry fee is paid and those entry fees become part of the purse. (Entry fees are not required for any other races.) Also invitational races (no entry fee required) with a large purse (usually $50,000 or more). All stakes can qualify a horse for black type in a sales catalog, and they are the highest class of race, above allowance races, overnight handicaps, and claiming races.

**STAKES ENGAGEMENTS:** The stakes races to which a horse has been nominated. Some stakes races have, as requirements, additional payments to maintain eligibility.

**STAKES-PLACED:** A horse that has finished second or third in a stakes race.

**STAKES-PRODUCER:** A mare that has produced at least one foal that finished first, second or third in a stakes race.

**STALLION:** A male horse that is used to produce foals.

**STANDARDBRED:** Pacers and trotters, these horses are a relatively new breed, dating back just 200 years. The term originated as the early trotters were required to reach a certain standard for the mile distance in order to be registered as part of the new breed.

**SUCKLING:** A foal that is still nursing.

**SYNDICATE:** A group of people who have formed an association usually for the purpose of allocating the breeding season of a particular stallion. One share, which can be sold or traded, usually gives the shareowner the right to breed one mare each breeding season to the syndicated stallion for as long as the stallion remains in service. Syndicates are formed because co-ownership divides the risk and expense of owning racehorses.

**TEASING:** A method using a stallion to court a mare to determine whether she is in heat and to encourage her to come into heat. Often farms have a stallion specifically for this purpose called a teaser, and he is usually not the stallion to whom the mare will be bred. The teaser will be led from mare to mare and if she is willing to be bred, certain physical changes will become apparent. If she is not in season, she will strongly rebuke the stallion's attentions, and it is for this reason that teaser's are used since one ill-placed kick from an irate mare can end a stallion's breeding career. A teaser can be of any breed, but usually should have a strong libido, be intelligent, and be manageable. Teasers are bred from time to time to nurse mares.

**THOROUGHBRED:** A breed of horse in North America registered with The Jockey Club. Not to be confused with purebred, which indicates an animal that is registered with any breed registry. All Thoroughbreds can trace their ancestry to three stallions: Darley Arabian, Godolphin Barb, and Byerly Turk.

**TRIPLE CROWN (Thoroughbred):** The three most important races for three-year-olds. In North America, it consists of the Kentucky Derby, Preakness Stakes, and Belmont Stakes. There have only been eleven Triple Crown winners: Sir Barton (1919), Gallant Fox (1930), Omaha (1935), War Admiral(1937), Whirlaway (1941), Count Fleet (1943), Assault (1946), Citation (1948), Secretariat (1973), Seattle Slew (1977) and Affirmed'(1978).

**TRIPLE CROWN (Trotting):** The three preeminent races in the trotting world, consisting of the Hambletonian, Kentucky Futurity, and Yonkers Trot. There have been six Triple Crown winners: Scott Frost (1955), Speedy Scot (1963), Ayres (1964), Nevele Pride (1968), Lindy's Pride (1969), and Super Bowl (1972).

**TROTTER:** A Standardbred that moves with a diagonal gait: the left front and right rear legs move in unison, as do the right front and left rear. It is a natural gait.

**TURF:** Grass as opposed to dirt racing surfaces. When capitalized, denotes the entire racing industry.

**TWO-YEAR-OLD:** A horse in its third calendar year of life, beginning January 1 of the year following its birth.

**WET MARE:** A mare with a foal of suckling age.

# Bibliography

"A Life of Sport and Service," The Blood-Horse, November 23,1991, p. 5564.

Alexander, David, A Sound of Horses, The Bobbs-Merrill Co., Inc., New York, 1966.

Beeler, Jaye, "Domino Stud, Mt. Brilliant Farms Sold to Guam Man," Lexington Herald-Leader, August 16,1989, pp. Al, A6, col. 1,.

Biles, Deirdre B., "John T. L. Jones Jr.," The Blood-Horse, August 13, 1988, p. 4578.

Blood-Horse, The, "It Was Kelso by a Neck at Laurel," August 18, 1990, p. 4266.

Bowen, Edward L. "All the Horseman's Kings," The Blood-Horse, August 8,1982, pp. 4684-4696.

Cady, Steve and Barton Silverman, Seattle Slew, Penguin Books, 1977.

Cooper, Jonathan, "John Henry," People Weekly, December 24-31, 1984, p. 97.

Cornett, Kip, "Welcome to EquiFestival of Kentucky," The Lane Report, September 1991, pp. 7-14.

de Moubray, Jocelyn, The Thoroughbred Business, Hamish Hamilton Press, London, Eng., 1987.

Deitel, Bob, "Unbridled Affection," The Courier-Journal, March 25, 1986, Accent, p. 1.

"Dixiana Broken Up By Sale; To Disperse Saddle Horses," Lexington Leader, June 5,1947, pp. Al, A8.

Duke, Jacqueline and Kevin Nance, "Horse Park Hits Stride After Years as Also-Ran," Lexington Herald-Leader, September 24,1988, Al.

Edwards, Don, "A Legacy of Timeless Glamour That Money Can't Buy," Lexington Herald-Leader, March 27,1992, A7, cols. 1-6.

Edwards, Don, "Chance Brought Horse Industry Here," The Lexington Leader, July 13,1984, A4, cols. 1-6.

"Five Great Breeders, " The American Trotter, pp. 314-319.

Flake, Carol, "The Killing Fields," Connoisseur, February 1992, pp. 48-51, 99-104.

"Getting There," The Blood-Horse, August 8,1981, pp. 4692-4696.

Harvey, Ellen and Moira Sullivan, "Women in Harness Racing," Hoof Beats, November 1988, pp. 31-34.

Herbert, Kimberly S., "Farm and Vet," The Blood-Horse, September 28,1991, p. 4628.

Hervey, John, The American Trotter, quoted by Tom White, "Walnut Hall Farm ... 'Out of the Farm, The Best,'" The Herald-Leader, February 1,1976, HI.

Hewitt, Abram S., The Great Breeders and Their Methods, Thoroughbred Publishers, Inc., Lexington, KY., 1982.

Hoffman, Dean A., "Walnut Hall Farm, 90 Years of Champions," Hoof Beats, September 1982, pp. 87-89.

Hollingsworth, Kent, The Wizard of the Turf, John E. Madden of Hamburg Place, Lexington, KY. 1965.

Jordan, Jim, "S. African Horseman Buying Greentree," Lexington Herald-Leader, May 13,1989, A9.

Kentucky Thoroughbred Farm Directory 1992, The Kentucky Thoroughbred Farm Manager's Club, Caddel &. Associates, Lexington, KY., 1992.

Malloy, Brian, "The Return of Nureyev," The Thoroughbred Record, March 1989, pp. 246-252.

Massie, Susanna, "Idle Hour's Outrageous Gambler," Bluegrass, May/ June 1988, Vol. Ill, No. 3, pp. 58-63.

Michelmore, P., "A Horse Named John Henry," The Reader's Digest, June 1985, vol. 126, pp. 151-160.

Mitchell, Ron, "Reaping the Benefits of Star Treatment," The Thoroughbred Times, August 12,1988, pp. 13-16.

Napier, Sue, "After Half-Century, Big Red Still Races in Realm of Legend," Sunday Herald-Leader, November 5, 1972, Al.

1991 Red Mile Grand Circuit Fact Book, Post Printing, Lexington, KY., 1991.

117th Kentucky Derby, Churchill Downs, May 4, 1991
Parker, Kathy, "Mrs. Katherine H. E. Nichols Dies," The Horseman and Fair World, December 3,1986, pp. 7-8.

Phelps, Frank T., "The Mostes' Hoss in Whole World," Lexington Leader, June 13, 1975.

Reed, Billy, "Man o' War, The greatest horse of his or any time?" Courier Journal, August 30,1976, p. Dl, cols. 1-6.

"Secretariat Called Winner in Simulated Horse Race," Wall Street Journal, December 12,1991, Eastern Edition, p. A6, col. 4.

Simpson, Elizabeth M., Bluegrass Houses and Their Traditions, Transylvania Press, Lexington, KY., 1932.

Simpson, Elizabeth M., The Enchanted Bluegrass, Transylvania Press, Lexington, KY., 1938.

Stroud, Joseph S., "Buyer Leads Lifestyle of Rich, Famous," Lexington Herald-Leader, March 27,1992, pp. Al, A10, col. 2-4.

Thoroughbred Racing and Sales 1992 Media Guide, Keeneland Association, Inc.

"$3 Million Horse Complex Planned by Dr. Pessin and Rex Ellsworth," Lexington Herald and Lexington Leader, September 20,1969, p. Al, cols. 3-6.

United States Trotting Association, A Primer on Harness Racing. Walghren, Sue, "Home, Sweet Horse Farm," Lexington Herald-Leader, June 21,1984, p. Dl.

Wharton, Mary E. and Edward L. Bowen, The Horse World of the Bluegrass, The John Bradford Press, Lexington, KY., 1980.

White, Jim, "Equine Impact Study," The Lane Report, September 1991, pp. 23-25.

White, Tom, "Walnut Hall Farm .. .'Out of the Farm, The Best,' Herald-Leader, February 1, 1976, p. HI.

Wilding, Suzanne and Anthony Del Balson, The Triple Crown Winners, Revised Edition, Parents' Magazine Press, New York, 1978.

Williams, Rhonda L., "Longhorn Horseman," Racing Times, December 2, 1991.

Wolfe, Jane, "The Winning Galbreaths," Town & Country Magazine, December 1985, pp. 207-215.

Young, Bennett H., A History of Jessamine County, Kentucky, Courier-Journal Printing Company, 1898.

# Endnotes

### Section 1 - Horse Farms of Note

1. Joseph S. Stroud, "Buyer Leads Lifestyle of Rich, Famous," Lexington Herald-Leader, March 27,1992, p. Al, col. 2-4.
2. Elizabeth M. Simpson, The Enchanted Bluegrass, Transylvania Press, Lexington, KY., 1938.
3. Kimberly S. Herbert, The Blood-Horse, "Farm and Vet," September 28,1991. p. 4628.
4. Brian Malloy, "The Return of Nureyev," The Thoroughbred Record, March 1989, pp. 246-252.
5. John Hervey, The American Trotter, quoted by Tom White, "Walnut Hall Farm ... 'Out of the Farm, The Best,'" The Herald-Leader, February 1,1976, p. HI.

### Section 2 - Horse Tales

1. Bennett H. Young, A History of Jessamine County, Kentucky, Courier-Journal Printing Company, 1898, p. 17.
2. Jonathan Cooper, "John Henry," People Weekly, December 24-31, 1984, p. 97.
3. Billy Reed, "Man o' War, The greatest horse of his ... or any time?'" Courier Journal, August 30,1976, p. Dl, cols. 1-6.
4. Ibid.
5. Elizabeth M. Simpson, The Enchanted Bluegrass, Transylvania Press, Lexington, KY., 1938.

# Index

800 - 849-08959

0159

Fein    Multimaster
        power tool

7 in 1   E Cut wood

         Grout Remo...

         Scrape

         Sanding